Kuṣāṇa Coins and History

Kuṣāṇa Coins and History

Parmeshwari Lal Gupta
Sarojini Kulashreshtha

DK PRINTWORLD
Publishers of Indian Traditions

Cataloging in Publication Data--DK
[Courtesy: D.K. Agencies (P) Ltd. <docinfo@dkagencies.com>]

Gupta, Parmeshwari Lal, 1914-2001, **author**.
Kuṣāṇa coins and history / Parmeshwari Lal Gupta, Sarojini Kulashreshtha. – Third impression.
pages cm
"First published in India in 1994" – Title page verso.
Includes bibliographical references and index.
ISBN 9788124600177

1. Coins, Kushan. 2. Kushans – History. 3. India – History – 324 BC - 1000 AD. I. Kulashreshtha, Sarojini, author. II. Title.

CJ3544.G87 2017 DDC 737.4934 23

ISBN 978-81-246-0017-7
First Published in India in 1994
Second impression in 2004
Third impression in 2017

Printed and published by
D.K. Printworld (P) Ltd.
Regd. Office : *'Vedaśrī'*, F-395, Sudarshan Park
(ESI Metro Station), New Delhi - 110 015
Phones : (011) 2545 3975; 2546 6019
e-mail : indology@dkprintworld.com
Web : www.dkprintworld.com

Introduction

THE Kuṣāṇas were the scion of a nomadic tribe from Central Asia, which were called by the Chinese as Yueh-chi. Coming out of their home-land some time during the third-second century B.C., they had gradually built up an extensive empire of their own that extended up to Central Asia in the west and the northern India in the east. For this, they are widely known in history. But what is known or written about them, are mainly based on the informations provided in the Chinese sources.

Information about them, in the Indian literary sources, is negligible. Amongst other Indian sources, that tell anything about them, are the inscriptions; they testify their existence in the Yamuno-Gangetic region. Numismatic materials are the other important sources for its political history. But their importance is not adequately realised and they seldom find references in the works of their history.

The Kuṣāṇa history had covered so far mainly only three rulers — Kaniṣka, Huviṣka and Vāsudeva, known from inscriptions, that are mainly dedicatory. They bear a date in an unspecified era along with the king's name and their epithets. The known dates begin with the year 2 and go up to the year 98. These dates are adjudged by the scholars as reckoned in the era of Kaniṣka (Kuṣāṇa).

Along with these three rulers, two others — Kaniṣka II and Vaśiṣka, were being suggested as co-rulers along with Ḥuviṣka and Vāsudeva on the basis of certain inscriptions, that have the dates that are considered as falling within the above period; the scholars had no other way to explain them.

At this early period, two other rulers — Kuzūla Kadphises and Vima Kadphises are placed before Kaniṣka. The existence of Kuzūla Kadphises, who is taken to be predecessor of Vima Kadphises, is not known outside Afghanistan towards India. It is only Vima Kadphises is taken as existing in the Yamuno-Gangetic region, exclusively on the basis of the finds of his coins. At the same time, it is also admitted that they had no relationship with the line of Kaniṣka.

On the other end, no date after the year 98 was known for any Kuṣāṇa ruler after Vāsudeva in the Kaniṣka's line; hardly any attention was paid to the coins, which appeared to have been issued by the rulers, who appeared to be Kuṣāṇas. They were taken almost non-entity in the context of the Yamuno-Gangetic region. Consequently, the historians felt a long gap in the history of this region after Kuṣāṇa Vāsudeva till the rise of the Gupta rulers in the fourth century A.D. Some attempts were made to patch up this gap with the presumptions that the Nāgas or the Yaudheyas might have occupied this region during this period of gap. But no serious attempt was ever made to probe into this vaccum.

With this background of the known Kuṣāṇa history, I considered from time-to-time, at intervals, during the span of about four decades (1959-89 A.D.), several problems related to the Kuṣāṇa history of the Northern India (Yamuno-Gangetic region) and wrote many articles. Later, Sarojini Kulashreshtha entered into the field and contributed some important papers. Here her two papers (papers 9-10) are bunched together with my ten papers (papers 1-8; 11-12); they focus attention mainly to the numismatic evidences and also keep in view all that are known from epigraphs. These papers, taken together, provide a new frame for the historians to work and look afresh at the Kuṣāṇa history. The problems that are dealt in these papers, in brief, are as follows:

1. So far, there had been nothing other than the coins to say the existence of Vima Kadphises in the Yamuno-Gangetic region. Now, attention has been drawn to an epigraph that indicates his existence. This inscription was discovered at Reh in the district of Fatehpur, Uttar Pradesh and is fragmentary. The

line that would have had the name of the king is lost (*fig. 31*). On wrong presumptions, it has been attributed to the Indo-Greek king Menander and cited as an evidence of his march towards Pāṭaliputra. Here, it is pointed out (paper 12) that all the epithets used in the inscription for the king, whose name is lost, were never used for that Indo-Greek king. They all apply, as a group, only to the Kuṣāṇa ruler Vima Kadphises; the inscription therefore, relates to his period and testify his presence in this region.

2. The gap between the period of Vima Kadphises and Kaniṣka is reduced partly by the discovery of a copper coin, found at Sonkh in Mathura district. The legend on the coin discloses that Kaniṣka was the son of hitherto unknown Huviṣka (Huviṣka I) (paper 5). The existence of a Huviṣka before Kaniṣka is substantiated here by isolating certain gold and copper coins that were so far believed to be the coins of Huviṣka, the successor of Kaniṣka. The existence of a Huviṣka, grand-father of the king of the same name, is mentioned in a Māṭ (Mathura) inscription. It also corroborates the coin evidences.

3. An important discovery dealt here (paper 12) is that the coins of Huviṣka, successor of Kaniṣka, other than those referred to above as the coins of Huviṣka I, the father of Kaniṣka, do not exclusively belong to one king named Huviṣka; but are related to two successive rulers of the same name, Huviṣka II and III (paper 12). The distinction between the coins of the two is pointed out and a similar instance is quoted from the coins of Indo-Śaka rulers named Azes. Supporting evidences are also quoted from several hoard-finds.

4. The inscriptions, on the basis of which joint rule of Vaśiṣka and Kaniṣka II in the period of Huviṣka and Vāsudeva was being presumed, do not belong to pre-Vāsudeva period. That myth is exploded here (papers 10 and 12). Those inscriptions belong to the post-Vāsudeva period and Vaśiṣka and Kaniṣka II actually existed in this period and they were in no way contemporaries of Huviṣka and Vāsudeva.

5. A break through the Kuṣāṇa history of the post-Vāsudeva

period, that had been in dark, was made by Lohuizen, an art historian, in 1948. She discovered some sculptures of Mathura that were stylistically distinct from the others. She thus showed that the Kuṣāṇa sculptures are of two series. When she discerned them, she found that many of them were inscribed and dated; and concluded that those sculptures, that are stylistically earlier, belong to pre-Vāsudeva period and the dates on them were reckoned in the Kaniṣka era. Those sculptures that are stylistically later, belong to post-Vāsudeva period and dates on them were in the continuity of the Kaniṣka era; but the figure of 100 was omitted. In other words, they had a new or Second Kuṣāṇa era. Her discovery, thus, brought to light some names of the rulers of this period. But her discovery remained ignored amongst the historians outside the field of art. Then Sarojini Kulashreshtha had made a break through from a quite different direction (paper 10). Discussing the coins of Vaśiṣka, she pointed out that those inscriptions, on the basis of which Vaśiṣka was being placed in the period of Huviṣka, bear an additional title *Ṣāhi* for Vaśiṣka along with the usual epithets of the Kuṣāṇa rulers *Ṣāhānuṣāhi Daivaputra*. And this additional epithet is also noticed on many of the inscriptions on those sculptures that Lohuizen had discerned on the stylistic considerations to the post-Vāsudeva period. She thus brought out a new evidence that leaves no doubt in the hundred-omitted or second Kuṣāṇa era after Vāsudeva. This also firmly establishes the existence of the Kuṣāṇa rule for almost half a century after Vāsudeva and provides a firm chronology for the rulers from him up to Kaniṣka III.

6. The Kuṣāṇas (*Daivaputra Ṣāhi Ṣāhānuṣāhi*) existed up to the time of the Gupta ruler Samudragupta; they existed along with another tribe or dynasty called Ṣaka (*Ṣaka-muruṇḍa*) as his neighbouring states. This was being suggested from a line in the Allahabad Pillar Inscription. A supporting evidence has now been found in certain coin-hoard that includes Kuṣāṇa coins along with coins of Samudragupta and Kācagupta (paper 8).

7. The finds of the coin-hoards also indicate that the Kuṣāṇas were deprived of the western part of their kingdom, the eastern

Indus region, that was left with them after they had lost their kingdom to the west of Indus to the Sassanids, to some tribal or dynastic rulers, that are called Tribal Kuṣāṇas for convenience (paper 8).

8. The Kidārites (Kidārs) ousted the Tribal Kuṣāṇa rulers from the territories, that they had snatched from the Kuṣāṇas, is equally evident from a hoard find. This might have happened in or about the time of the Gupta ruler Candragupta II. It is also suggested on the basis of another hoard-find that Skandagupta had led an army expedition against them (paper 8). Most likely, these Kidārites (Kidārs) are referred to as *Mleccha* in his Junagarh inscription.

9. In four papers, taken together (papers 8-11) attempt has been made and reasonably successfully, to show that the Kuṣāṇas existed for about 100 years more after Vāsudeva had lost a part of his kingdom to the Sassanids. But they did not have the entire kingdom that was now left, for this entire period of 100 years. At some period they also lost some western parts; only the Yamuno-Gangetic region was left with them till the end. They were extinguished from there by the Gupta ruler Candragupta II in *circa* 370 A.D.

10. One of the most vexed problem of the Kuṣāṇa history, had been before the scholars for the last two centuries, is the beginning of Kaniṣka's rule, i.e., the Kuṣāṇa era. In the early days of the controversy at least nine theories were current. Every scholar, who touched the problem, believed that his scheme would solve the problem; but none of them had any acceptance. Consequently, a colloquium was organised by the Royal Asiatic Society, London in 1913 to thrash out the problem. As the results of the discussions there, two dates 58 B.C. (Vikrama era) and 78 A.D. (Śaka era) came to the fore. In later days, none seemed serious about the former; but the later found acceptance with most of the scholars. Even that did not have the general acceptance. From time-to-time, scholars came out with new dates, running over second and third centuries A.D. One of scholars, who places Kaniṣka in the third century A.D., argued his date placing an

evidence of a Romano-Kuṣāṇa medallion in the British Museum. The absurdity of this evidence is exposed here in one of the papers (paper 7). I, myself, place the beginning of the Kaniṣka (Kuṣāṇa) era in the fifth decade of the second century A.D. I expressed my views first in 1960 at the Colloquium organised at the School of Oriental and African Studies (London University). In that Colloquium I dwelt the subject in the light of the political conditions that was existing at the time when the Kuṣāṇas entered into the Yamuno-Gangetic region. I pointed out to the presence of the rulers of local dynasties at Mathura, Pañcāla, Kauśāmbī and Ayodhyā in the post-Mauryan period. I calculated their reign periods and came to the conclusion that 144 A.D. as the probable date for the Kuṣāṇa's entry in this region. This date was the same, that was earlier suggested by Ghirshman on the basis of his excavations at Begram (Afghanistan) (paper 4). Subsequently, in three other papers, (papers 8, 11 and 12) I touched the subject again. At this time, I held the thread from the other end. I placed the firm date of the extinction of the Kuṣāṇas from the Mathura region in the time of Gupta ruler Candragupta II in *circa* 370 A.D. Calculating back 120 years for the post-Vāsudeva Kuṣāṇa rulers now known, postulated the beginning of the Kuṣāṇa era in *circa* 150 A.D. (370 - (120 + 100). The dates 144 and 150 A.D., proposed by me earlier, are by no means precise or absolute; nevertheless, they are less hypothetical than any other date so far suggested and hold firm grounds.

11. The extension of the Kuṣāṇa kingdom in the east, had hardly been any consideration with the historians; only a few numismatic scholars has been enthusiast about it. They tried to put together all that they can lay in their hands in the name of numismatics to show that Uttar Pradesh, Bihar, Orissa and the Gangetic Delta of Bengal were included for some time within the empire of Kaniṣka. I have critically examined all these materials, laid down to suggest this conclusion, and refuted their validity (articles 1, 2 and 3). I was quite new to the field when I wrote the first two papers, nevertheless, I tried to expose the hollowness of the suggestion. I maintained that the Kuṣāṇa kingdom did never extended beyond Vārāṇasī in the east. In a

later paper (paper 6), I scrutinised all the material that was laid down to show the eastern expansion of the Kuṣāṇa kingdom, afresh and reiterated my original view that the Kuṣāṇas never crossed the Gaṅgā beyond Vārāṇasī. The coins and the other numismatic objects known in those areas, were no evidence of the Kuṣāṇa rule over there. They are found in those areas, only because they had reached through trade; and that too, not as any currency but merely as the commodities of common need during the time of the Guptas, who had hardly any copper coinage and people needed it to meet their petty needs.

These investigations, scattered in these papers, though worked out at long intervals, in their totality, throw fresh light on the history of the Kuṣāṇas from their rise in the mid-second century A.D. till their doom in the mid of the fourth century A.D., after their existence for two centuries in the Yamuno-Gangetic region. Hope, they would stimulate the re-thinking of the historians and would provide them a new frame to re-write the Kuṣāṇa history. I very much desire that readers would dispassionately take note of the merit of these papers, whatever they might worth.

May 2, 1994 **Parmeshwari Lal Gupta**

Indian Institute of Research
in Numismatic Studies,
Anjaneri, 422 213
Nasik (Maharashtra)

Acknowledgements

We acknowledge with thanks the permission accorded by the Numismatic Society of India, Varanasi (Papers 2, 3, 5, 6 and 7), Indian Institute of Research in Numismatic Studies, Anjaneri, Nasik (Papers 9 and 10), K.P. Jayaswal Research Institute, Patna (Paper 8), American Institute of Indian Studies, New Delhi (Paper 11), Instituto Universitario Oreintale, Naples (Italy) (Paper 12) and E.J. Brill, Leiden (Netherlands) (Paper 4) to include the papers mentioned against their names in this volume.

Paper 1 was published in *Indian Historical Quarterly* (Calcutta), which has ceased its existence for a quite long time. It is included here with apologies to who-so-ever might have any claim over that Journal.

Authors

Contents

Abbreviations

A.B.O.R.I.	*Annals of Bhandarkar Oriental Research Institute, Pune.*
A.S.I., A.R.	*Archaeological Survey of India, Annual Report.*
A.S.M.B.	*Asiatic Society, Monthly Bulletin, Calcutta.*
B.M.A.U.P.	*Bulletin Museums & Archaeology, Uttar Pradesh.*
B.M.C., A.I.	*British Museum Catalogue of Coins, Ancient India.*
B.S.O.A.S.	*Bulletin of the School of Oriental & African Studies, London.*
C.A.S.R.	*Cunningham, Archaeological Survey Report.*
E.I.	*Epigraphia Indica.*
I.A.	*Indian Antiquary.*
I.C.	*Indian Culture, Calcutta.*
I.H.Q.	*Indian Historical Quarterly, Calcutta.*
I.M.B.	*Indian Museum Bulletin, Calcutta.*
I.N.C.	*Indian Numismatic Chronicle, Patna.*
J.A.	*Journale Asiatique, Paris.*
J.A.O.S.	*Journal of American Oriental Society, New York.*
J.A.S.B.	*Journal of Asiatic Society, Bengal, Calcutta.*
J.B.O.R.S.	*Journal of Bihar & Orissa Research Society, Patna.*
J.E.S.I.	*Journal of Epigraphical Society of India.*
J.N.S.I.	*Journal of the Numismatic Society of India, Varanasi.*

J.R.A.S.	*Journal of Royal Asiatic Society, London.*
J.U.P.H.S.	*Journal of U.P. Historical Society, Lucknow.*
M.J.L.S.	*Madras Journal of Letters & Science, Madras.*
N.D.	*Numismatic Digest, Nasik.*
O.H.R.J.	*Orissa Historical Research Journal, Bhubaneswar.*
P.A.I.O.C.	*Proceedings, All-India Oriental Conference.*
P.A.S.B.	*Proceedings, Asiatic Society of Bengal, Calcutta.*
P.J.A.S.B.	*Proceedings & Journal Asiatic Society of Bengal, Calcutta.*
P.M.C.	*Punjab Museum Catalogue of Coins: I, Indo-Greeks & others, Lahore.*
T.I.N.C.	*Transactions of the International Numismatic Congress.*

List of Illustrations

1

Eastern Expansion of the Kuṣāṇa Empire*

INSPIRED with the suggestion of A. S. Altekar, who had published a hoard of Kuṣāṇa coins from Buxar in Bihar and had suggested that Magadha was conquered by the Kuṣāṇas early in their dynastic history in the time of Vima Kadphises and they lost their hold over it towards the end of the reign of Huviṣka,[1] Adris Banerji has collected numismatic, epigraphic and sculptural data, under the above caption[2] to show that U.P., Bihar and possibly the Gangetic delta in Bengal, as well as Orissa were included for a time within the empire of Kaniṣka. While the paper is interesting, a careful, balanced, unbiased and fair study of the available materials would show that there is hardly anything to weave out any such possibilities.

Banerji has referred to the following inscriptions, pointing out that they specifically mention the name of Kaniṣka in Eastern India:

1. Inscription on a Buddha image at Sārnāth.
2. Inscription on a Buddha image found at Sahet-Mahet, (ancient Śrāvastī).
3. Inscription on an image found at Gayā by Cunningham.

To this list of Banerji, I would add one more inscription found on a Buddha image at Kosam, ancient Kauśāmbī,[3] which, he did not include in the list. But at the same time, the image

* Originally published in *Indian Historical Quarterly*, XXIX. 3, (1953), pp. 205-221.

which is said by Banerji to have been found by Cunningham at Gaya has nothing by the way of reference to Kaniṣka or any other Kuṣāṇa king, and has no value in the present context. As a matter of fact Banerji, himself, is not sure if the image has any such thing. Though he has quoted Cunningham's *Mahābodhī* as the authority of his assertion, he did not consult the book. He seems to have relied on B. C. Sen, whose name he has mentioned in the footnote.[4] I have consulted the *Mahābodhī*, but I failed to find any reference to any such image which has got any inscription mentioning the name of Kaniṣka or any other Kuṣāṇa king. There is one Buddha image with the inscription dated in the 64th year of a king named Trikamala. This image is no doubt assigned to the Kuṣāṇa period by Cunningham, but artistically it is doubtful if it could be assigned to that period. In all probability it belongs to the later part of the third century A.D. But even if it be taken as belonging to Kuṣāṇa period, it shows that there was some independent kingdom in Bihar during the Kuṣāṇa period, and it was not under the domination of the Kuṣāṇas.

Having excluded this inscription from the list, we have nothing coming from Bihar, which specifically mentions the name of Kaniṣka or any other Kuṣāṇa king, suggesting Kuṣāṇa hold over the territory. The other three inscriptions are confined to eastern U.P. and they do not suggest anything Kuṣāṇa beyond Banaras, if the find-spots be taken as a conclusive evidence on this point. We shall discuss these inscriptions a little later.

Banerji has given next, a list of inscriptions that are found in Bihar and have Kuṣāṇa characters. Script called Kuṣāṇa, on any inscription found at any place in Bihar or anywhere else, does not suggest any political domination. It is just a name to indicate the developed form of the letters that are found in the period when Kuṣāṇas were the main ruler in a part of the country. Moreover, the inscriptions listed by Banerji are engraved on images which are made of red sand-stone of Karrā (Agra) and the style as well as the technique of these images betray their production from Mathura studio. There is no doubt that these images were imported from Mathura to the localities where they have been found. Therefore, it is no wonder if they have Kuṣāṇa script on them. An imported article is in no way a sure indication of political domination of the place, where it is found, under the ruler of the place of the origin of that article.

But Banerji has pointed out that the Rajmahal slate was used in sculptures in Eastern India in various periods; but not in the Kuṣāṇa period. In this period only the red sand-stone of Karrā is found, which disappears with the disintegration of the Kuṣāṇa empire. 'In Gupta period', he says, 'the studios of Mathura were still working, but the red sand-stone of Mathura remains within the limits of the Doab between the Gaṅgā and the Yamunā; and never again to reappear on the soil of eastern India in the wake of other empires that followed that of the Kuṣāṇas'. Banerji wants to impress upon us that in spite of the local stone, if images of stones of a particular place is imported in a particular period, it is a sure indication of the political domination. To him, the presence of Mathura stone, in spite of Rajmahal stone in Bihar, indicates the Kuṣāṇa occupation of that province.

It is a matter of common knowledge that the Indian art during the Kuṣāṇa period developed in Gandhāra and Mathura only. No local art is known flourishing at Banaras and Magadha. Had there been so, we would naturally have had some specimens of that art in the local Chunār and Rajmahal stones. But when in the Gupta period, Banaras developed its own school of art, we find sculptures of Chunār sand-stone in eastern U.P. and Bihar in abundance. People, naturally, did not feel necessity anymore to import stone images from distant places like Mathura. Even in this period, we do not have Rajmahal stones used in sculptures of Magadha, since art was not till then developed in that area. Had there been any such thing, as Banerji postulates with the presence of Mathura stones at Bihar, we would surely have had Chunār stone images in abundance at Mathura and other places, with the advent of the Gupta domination in that area. But such is not the case. So, one can naturally infer that in the Kuṣāṇa period, when the eastern India lacked an art of its own, out of love for the religion or by way of curiosity of introducing new things in their own land, people imported images from the known centre of their manufacture at Mathura. But when they developed their own art, they ceased to import. It is well apparent by the very fact that we have a few images of Mathura in Bihar and eastern U.P. As such, it is just an imagination to suggest any political reason behind their presence in Bihar. There is hardly anything by the way of art and inscriptions to show the extant of Kuṣāṇa empire in Bihar.

Now, coming to the Kuṣāṇa occupation in the eastern U.P. we have, no doubt, as pointed out above, three inscribed Buddha images, that are found at Kauśāmbī, Sāranāth and Śrāvastī and bear the name of Kaniṣka. These inscriptions seem to suggest Kaniṣka's rule, extending up to Banaras, and not only Banerji, but many scholars share this view. But the tragedy had been with the scholars that they have always ignored Kauśāmbī and Śrāvastī inscriptions and have laid stress only on the Sārnāth inscription. If the three images and their inscriptions are studied together, we shall see that they are not the least connected with the empire of Kaniṣka.

All the three images are made of Karrā red sand-stone and are the products most likely of a single artist of Mathura school. They are strikingly similar in style and workmanship. Their inscriptions are also similar in nature, language and script. One of them (Kauśāmbī image) is dated in the 2nd year of Kaniṣka, the other (Sārnāth image) is dated in the third year of his reign; on the third, (Śrāvastī image) unfortunately the date is damaged, but it is also in the year of the reign of Kaniṣka. The donor of the Śrāvastī image was friar Bala the follower of friar Puṣyavuddhi and that of Kauśāmbī, friar Bala's disciple nun Buddhamitrā. The Sārnāth image is a joint donation of the two, i.e., friar Bala and nun Buddhamitrā. These two Buddhists are again mentioned on the inscribed Bodhisattva image from Mathura, preserved in Lucknow Museum, dated in the year 33 in the reign of Huviṣka. This image was the gift of nun Dhanavatī, the sister's daughter of Tripiṭaka Buddhamitrā, the disciple of the Tripiṭaka Bala.[5] It is clear from this, that the three inscriptions belonged to these two persons, who were beyond doubt on pilgrimage and were not the inhabitants of either of the three places Kauśāmbī, Sārnāth and Śrāvastī and most likely they had come from Mathura and had brought with them the images to install on the occasion of their pilgrimage at the sacred sites of Buddhism. As such they too do not have anything which may be interpreted as an evidence of Kaniṣka's hold over these places.

But the two names Kharapallana and Vanaspara, which are mentioned in the Sārnāth image inscription with the titles Mahākṣatrapa and Kṣatrapa respectively, have made the scholars imaginative and they think that they were viceroy and governor at Banaras at that time under Kaniṣka. But this inference is never warranted from the lines of the inscriptions, which are as follows:

1. भिक्षुस्य बलस्य त्रेपिटकस्य बोधिसत्त्वो छत्रयष्ठि प्रतिष्ठापितो वाराणसिये भगवतो चंकमे सहा माता पितिहि सहा उपद्धयायाचर्येहि सद्धयेविहारिहि अंतेवासिकेहि च सहा बुद्धमित्रये त्रेपिटिकये सहा क्षत्रपेण वनस्परेन खरपल्लानेन च सहा च चतुहि परिषाहि सर्वसत्वनं हितासुखार्थं ।
2. भिक्षुस्य बलस्यत्रेपिटकस्य बोधिसत्त्वो प्रतिष्ठापितो महाक्षत्रपेन खरपल्लानेन सहा क्षत्रपेन बनस्परेन ।

In these two inscriptions the name of the two Kṣatrapas are mentioned clearly as the associates in the donation of the statue of the Bodhisattva and the umbrella, in the same way as is mentioned the name of the nun Buddhamitrā. There is nothing to indicate that Kharapallana and Vanaspara were stationed at Banaras in any administrative capacity. At the best it can only be inferred that they were also pilgrims like the friar Bala and nun Buddhamitrā and in all probability they accompanied them in their journey and shared in the said donation.

But much colour has been given to the imagination by Jayaswal, who suggested that a Kṣatriya tribe was known as Banāphara in Bundelkhand and they were the descendants of this Vanaspara and a dialect is still known there as Banāpharī.

Banerji has quoted George Grierson to suggest that they had their home originally at Buxar. But it is incorrect to say that Banāphara Rajputs are the original inhabitants of Bihar. They have migrated to this area within the recent centuries from the west. We also do not have any tradition among the Banāphara Rajputs to suggest that they are the descendants of Vanaspara. The *Paurāṇic* tradition places Vanaspara at Padmāvatī, if he is the same as Vinvasphāṇī, Vimbsphāti, or Visvaphāṇi, as suggested by Jayaswal.

Banerji considers the reference of the Kaniṣka era in these inscriptions, as the crucial point in the matter. To him the use of the reckoning started by Kaniṣka, in an area, where he had no political interest, seems to be most amazing. So, to emphasise that Kaniṣka era would not have been used in these inscriptions, had the territory not been under him, he has cited instances showing that kings did not use their own era or reign period, when they erected monuments outside their own kingdom. Kings might or might not have used their era or reign period outside their kingdoms; it has no bearing on the present question. It seems Banerji has ignored the fact that none of the present inscriptions are the official records of the Kuṣāṇa kings. He has cited no injunction against people at large, banning the use of the dates of their own choice on their records.

However, if these territories were under the Kuṣāṇas, it is most amazing to get only these three inscriptions dated in the beginning of the Kaniṣka era; and that too, used by a single group of men, when we get hundreds of inscriptions from Mathura and other parts of the Kuṣāṇa kingdom, dated in the reign of Kaniṣka, Huviṣka and other kings and in Kuṣāṇa era. It is not that we do not have inscriptions in the Kuṣāṇa script in this area. The inscriptions of this period are well-known from Kauśāmbī, Bandhogarh, Ahicchatrā etc., but none of them refer to Kuṣāṇa kings. Thus it is very doubtful if ever this area was under the Kuṣāṇas.

But before any judgment is pronounced in this matter, it is necessary that the local history of Kauśāmbī, Pañcāla, and

Ayodhyā be examined critically, which is unfortunately so far ignored.[6]

The numismatic material that have come to light from Kauśāmbī in recent days shows that Vavaghoṣa and Aśvaghoṣa were ruling there towards the end of the third century B.C. They were most probably followed by Parvata and Sudeva. These kings were followed by the kings of Mitra dynasty towards the end of second century B.C. Beginning from the king Mitra, this dynasty included at least 15 kings Rādhamitra, Agnimitra, Jyeṣṭhamitra, Bṛhaspatimitra, Suramitra, Varuṇamitra, Poṭhamitra, Sarpamitra, Prajāpatimitra, Satyamitra, Rājamitra, Rajnīmitra, Devamitra, Īśvaramitra, and Śivamitra.[7] These were supplanted by the kings of Magha dynasty. Bhadramagha, Śivamagha, Bhīmavarman, Satamagha, Vijayamagha, Puramagha, Yugamagha, Nāvika, Puṣvaśrī, Dhanadeva, are the 10 kings of this period known from their coins. The last ruler of Kauśāmbī was Rudra, who was subdued by Samudragupta and is mentioned as Rudradeva in the Allahabad pillar inscription. The coins of all these kings are purely local and have no influence of the Kuṣāṇa or any other coinage, to suggest that they were feudatories under them. Thus from the end of the second century B.C. to the middle of the fourth century A.D. Kauśāmbī was ruled continuously by local rulers, independent of any imperial pressure. Still we get there the Buddha image with inscription dated in the reign of Kaniṣka, which suggests nothing but the donor belonged to the territory of Kaniṣka and not that the territory was under Kaniṣka.

Now turning towards Pañcāla, we find a long series of uniform coinage with no less than twenty-two kings, viz. Rūdragupta, Jayagupta, Dāmagupta, Vaṅgapāla, Viśvapāla, Yajñapāla, Vasusena, Sūryamitra, Dhruvamitra, Viṣṇumitra, Indramitra, Agnimitra, Varuṇamitra, Prajāpatimitra, Bhānumitra, Bhūmimitra, Jayamitra, Phālgunīmitra, Aṇumitra, Āyumitra and Bṛhaspatimitra.[8] The beginning of this kingdom is believed to be the end of the third century B.C. These twenty-two kings must have ruled for no less than five centuries, i.e., up to third century A.D. or to the rise of the Guptas. Here too the coinage is purely local and has no foreign influence. There is nothing to suggest that they were the feudatories of the Kuṣāṇas. Thus it is clear that Pañcāla was also an independent kingdom during the reign of the Kuṣāṇas.

The third kingdom of Ayodhyā (Kosala), which lies in between these two kingdoms had all along a very unsettled state. Some time it formed part of Pañcāla and at the other of Kauśāmbī. But at occasions it also asserted its own independence. Though it lacks the smoothness that we find in the history of Kauśāmbī and Pañcāla, still there is nothing to suggest that it ever acknowledged the suzerainty of the Kuṣāṇas. Ayodhyā (Kosala), as an independent kingdom, most probably came into existence after Puṣyamitra Śuṅga in the latter half of the second century B.C. And since then we have here the kings Mūladeva, Vāyudeva, Viśākhadeva, Phālgunīdeva, Dhanadeva, Śivadatta, Naradatta, Jyeṣṭhadatta, Satyamitra, Devamitra, Āryamitra, Saṅghamitra, Vijayamitra, Kumudasena and Ajavarman.[9] The list does not seem complete. There may be a few more kings, with the interregnums of the Kauśāmbī and Pañcāla rules. But even this list of 15 names shows that they would have ruled up to the end of second century A.D., and they may even go up to third century A.D. if a proper history is constructed. The coins of these kings too are free from foreign influence and do not suggest any Kuṣāṇa domination.

Thus the reconstructed history of Kauśāmbī, Pañcāla and Ayodhyā shows that they were independent kingdoms, when the Kuṣāṇas were ruling at Mathura. The Kuṣāṇas could have proceeded to Banaras and Magadha, only if anyone of these was subdued, for which we have still no evidence. What we have at present suggests that Kuṣāṇa empire was extended at the most up to Kānyakubja in the east.

But Banerji and Altekar put before us a long list of the finds of Kuṣāṇa coins widely scattered in Bengal, Orissa, Bihar and eastern U.P. They vehemently advocate that these coins are conclusive evidence of Kuṣāṇa expansion in the east. No doubt, in view of the numismatic axiom – copper coins do not travel generally long outside the territory of their circulation – *prima facie*, there is every justification for the conclusions in the favour of the extension of the Kuṣāṇa empire to Magadha and even beyond. But at the same time we cannot undervalue the history of Kauśāmbī, Pañcāla and Ayodhyā, reconstructed on the basis of numismatic and other evidences.

So this material needs a critical examination, before we reach at any conclusion.

Banerji has given the following list of the finds in Bengal:

(i) A copper coin of Kaniṣka, found in 1882 at Tāmluk in Midnapur district.

(ii) A base metal coin of Vāsudeva found in 1890 in Murshidabad district.

(iii) A gold coin of Vāsudeva, found in 1909 in Bogra district.

(iv) Three Kuṣāṇa coins from North Bengal. Two of them came from Mahāsthān and one of them belonged to Vāsudeva, and the other is not assigned to any particular king. The third coin hailed from Malda and belonged to Vāsudeva. (Banerji has mentioned these coins as silver pieces. But no silver coin from this area is ever known of this dynasty).

Of the four entries of the list, three refer to non-copper coinage belonging to Vāsudeva. Gold and silver coins may travel far and off from their place of origin by way of trade. So one can well suggest that they came to Bengal by that way. Moreover, there is hardly anyone, who thinks that Vāsudeva had ever ruled as far as Bengal. He is not considered to have such an extensive area under him. So, on the basis of a single copper coin found at Tāmluk, an ancient port of international importance, it seems idle to suggest that Bengal was under the Kuṣāṇas, for any amount of period.

Next, following is the list of finds from Orissa given by Banerji:

(i) Copper coins of Kaniṣka and Huviṣka were found at Bhañjikā in Mayurabhanj district. (This hoard was found in 1923 and included the coins of Purī-Kuṣāṇa type, in which some of them were inscribed.[10])

(ii) 112 copper coins of Great Kuṣāṇas were found at Mayurabhanj by R. D. Banerji. (This hoard was found probably in 1923 or 1924, but the find-spot is not recorded. This hoard also included 170 Purī-Kuṣāṇa coins.[11])

(iii) Kuṣāṇa coins were found in the excavations of Virāṭgarh in Mayurabhanj district. (P. Acharya informs that a few Kuṣāṇa coins were found with a large number of Purī-Kuṣāṇa coins.[12])

(iv) Copper coins of Kaniṣka and Huviṣka were found at Śiśupālagarh. (Only one coin each of the two kings were found in the excavations, with four coins of Purī-Kuṣāṇas. These have been found in the later level which may be dated according to the excavation report to 300-350 A.D.[13])

The information given above within brackets is added by me. They show that none of the Kuṣāṇa coins known from Orissa, were found independent of the Purī-Kuṣāṇa coins. The Bhañjikā hoard had some inscribed coins, with the legends in the characters of the fourth century A.D.[14] It is therefore clear that the coins were not deposited earlier than that period. The excavation report of Śiśupālagarh informs that the Kaniṣka coin was found worn on the late unstratified layer and the coin of Huviṣka, which was in a fair condition was found in the upper level of the period II B, i.e., dating towards the end of the second century A.D.[15]

It is clear from these coins that they were current in Orissa in the period, when the Kuṣāṇa empire has ceased to exist in the North India. So there arises no question of their domination over this area.

Now we come to Bihar. Banerji records three finds from this province.

(i) A gold coin of Huviṣka was found in Belwadaga thana and a copper coin of Kaniṣka in the Karra thana of the Ranchi district.

(ii) Excavations at Pāṭaliputra yielded two copper coins of Kaniṣka and more of Vima Kadphises and Huviṣka. (Altekar has recently published the list of the coins which were found in the Pāṭaliputra excavations and Bulandībāgh in 1912-13. He gives the number of the coins as Vima Kadphises 3, Kaniṣka 12, and Huviṣka 30.[16])

(iii) Kuṣāṇa coins have been found at Vaiśālī in large number.

To this list should be added the Buxar hoard, which Altekar has recently published and on which he has built up his theory of the Kuṣāṇa occupation of Magadha.

(iv) Buxar hoard included copper coins; of them 23 are of Vima Kadphises, 159 of Kaniṣka and 172 of Huviṣka, 38 undecipherable and 10 Ayodhyā coins of Bull and Cock series, i.e., the coins of Mitra kings.[17]

Lastly, I would add one more find.

(v) Ganesh Chaube of Bangari, district Champaran, sent me in 1952 a few copper Kuṣāṇa coins, collected from his area. They included a coin of Vima Kadphises and the rest were of Huviṣka.

Of these finds, the coins found in the excavations at Pāṭaliputra and Vaiśālī would have been valuable evidence had their stratification been properly recorded. Altekar has pointed out that square and round cast coins were found in large number in the Kumrahāra excavations. He concludes that this tends to show that the copper currency of the Kuṣāṇa succeeded in completely ousting the indigenous copper currency of cast coins. This, he says, took place in about 75 A.D.[18] But in absence of the stratification, there is nothing positive to suggest such an hypothesis. I have just pointed out above that the Śiśupālagarh excavations give the date of currency of the Kuṣāṇa coins at about 200 A.D. There too, cast coins were found and they suggest that they were in currency from 50 A.D. to 350 A.D. Three of the coins, out of total nine, were found in the upper layer of Period IIA attributable to *c.* A.D. 50-100, the same number were found in the early level of period IIB, datable to 100-125 A.D. and the remaining three were obtained from later deposits which may be assigned to 200-350 A.D.[19] The coin of Huviṣka, here was found in the upper level of period IIB, datable to about 200 A.D. The cast coins were current in second and third century A.D. is also borne out from a hoard of coins from Kauśāmbī, which includes square cast coins with the coins of Maghas. Same might have been the case in Magadha also; and the Kuṣāṇa coins might have followed the cast coins. However, in absence of any definite knowledge about the level of their finds, we cannot attach any importance to the finds of the excavations of Pāṭaliputra and Vaiśālī, for determining the period of their currency.

The Buxar hoard should be assessed on its own merit of being an intact one. But before doing so, I would like to enlist the hoards that are known from the eastern U.P.:

1. 105 Kuṣāṇa copper coins were found at Sahet-Mahet in the cell of a monastery in the excavations of 1908-9. It included 2 coins of Kaniṣka, 2 of Huviṣka, 96 of Vāsudeva and the remaining were badly effaced.[20]
2. 100 copper Kuṣāṇa coins were found in the village Bindwal in Azamgarh district in 1949-50 and the kings represented there were Kaniṣka and Huviṣka.[21]
3. A hoard of Kuṣāṇa coins was found on the bank of a *nālā* in the village Nai in the district of Azamgarh in or about 1938; but it is nowhere recorded. A few coins were brought to me from a resident of that village, which suggested that the hoard included the coins of Kaniṣka and Huviṣka and Cock and Bull type coins of Ayodhyā.
4. A big hoard of several hundred coins were found at Ṣidhāri, on the outskirt of Azamgarh town in or about 1950 A.D. while a trench was being made for the foundation of a house. This hoard is also unrecorded, but a portion of it formed part of the collection of Ramashanker Rawat of Azamgarh. Most of the coins were of Kaniṣka and Huviṣka. It also included a few Ayodhyā coins of Cock and Bull type.

Of the five hoards listed above, (three from Azamgarh district, and one each from Sahet-Mahet and Buxar) at least three have a common feature that the Kuṣāṇa coins were found mixed with the Ayodhyā coins of Bull and Cock type. These Ayodhyā coins are comparatively few in number in all these hoards. According to the axiom of numismatics, they show that either they were issued earlier than Kuṣāṇa coins or after them. Altekar was of the opinion that the Mitra kings of Ayodhyā, who issued these coins were most probably slightly later than the time of Kaniṣka and Vāsudeva. He places them in the second century A.D., and suggests that they probably ruled as the feudatories of the Kuṣāṇas and were allowed to issue coins.[22]

India knows three big empires, during the historical period of 2500 years, viz. Nanda-Maurya, Gupta and Mughal. The coinage of Nanda-Maurya (i.e., Punch-marked coins) is still enigmatic to the numismatists; but we know much about the other two empires. We know not a single example where the emperors of these empires, had allowed their feudatories to issue their own coinage. The later Mughals, during the period of the decadence of the empire, had tolerated the minting of the coins by their feduatories, but the feudatories never dared to issue coins in their own name. Altekar himself has admitted that no Gupta feudatory was ever permitted to mint any coins.[23] I wonder then how he took that the Kuṣāṇas would have permitted a feudatory family ruling at Ayodhyā to issue its own coinage. But even if we presume that they did permit the minting to their Ayodhyā feudatories, how is that we do not find any Kuṣāṇa influence over these coins? If the Ayodhyā feudatories issued their own coins, it is natural to expect that their coins would have been more in currency than that of the Kuṣāṇas, being local currency. In our own times, we had many Indian states, under the British rule, who were issuing their own coins, within their own territory. They can well be placed to the analogy of the situation in Ayodhyā under the Kuṣāṇas. Here in Hyderabad or Gwalior, the two principal states of our times issued their own coins, we had always found their own coins current along with the British currency; the former being more frequent than those of the British overlords. Therefore, if not more, at least in a sufficient number the Ayodhyā coins ought to have been found in these hoards as they were found in the heart of the Ayodhyā kingdom. In absence of any such evidence, the suggestion of Kuṣāṇa domination of Ayodhyā during the reign of Mitra kings is an improbability.

However, it may be assumed that Mitra kings were formerly feudatories of the Kuṣāṇas during the height of that empire. In that period they did not issue their own coins. But on its fall when they became independent they issued their own coins. This may well account for the constitution of the hoards. But we have nothing to show that Mitra coins dated to the period after the Kuṣāṇas. They cannot in any case be placed later than second century A.D. We have nothing to reconcile with the fact that Mitra coinage supplanted the Kuṣāṇa coinage at Buxar immediately after Huviṣka and at Sahet-Mahet, their own principal town, Vāsudeva continued to rule, the situation which appears from the hoards found at respective places. To meet this awkward situation, one may possibly suggest that Mitras rose at Bihar on the ruins of the Kuṣāṇas after Huviṣka and later they occupied Ayodhyā after Vāsudeva. But for this suggestion too, we have no evidence. The study of the coinage of Ayodhyā and Kauśāmbī, with the view of reconstruction of the local history, shows that the Mitras of Ayodhyā were the off-shoots of the Kauśāmbī dynasty, which remained confined to Ayodhyā and flourished within first two centuries of the Christian era.

So, there is nothing for the present to sugegst the contemporaneity of the Mitra kings of Ayodhyā with the Kuṣāṇa kings or their posteriority to them. The numismatic evidences place them earlier than the Kuṣāṇas, i.e., the Mitra coins were followed by the Kuṣāṇa coins in the later part of second century A.D. in this area. We arrive at this very conclusion from the evidence of Śiśupālagarh excavations also.

The rise of Kaniṣka is generally believed in 78 A.D.[24] and his dynasty ruled in this country for about 100 years, after which his great empire passed away. Accordingly, by the end of second century A.D. the Kuṣāṇas did not exist in northern India. The available material discussed above suggests that no coins of the Kuṣāṇas were current within first-second century A.D. in eastern U.P., Bihar and Orissa, which ultimately means that the Kuṣāṇas had no hold over these territories. The coins came into currency in this part of the country after their fall.

But it may be pointed out here that copper coins generally do not travel long outside the territory of their circulation. As such the coins seem to suggest that Kuṣāṇas might exist in these areas, in the later part of the second and third century A.D. Though inscriptional and sculptural evidences are lacking, as shown above, for the existence of the Kuṣāṇas in these areas, the Chinese and Tibetan traditions suggest the Kuṣāṇa occupation of eastern U.P. and Magadha. They record Kaniṣka's war with Sāket and Pāṭaliputra. If it was so, the generally accepted date of 78 A.D. for the rise of Kaniṣka, will have to be reviewed in the light of these evidences. There has been suggestions for Kaniṣka's reign in second century A.D. It has been pointed out by scholars that the downfall of the Kuṣāṇa empire was mainly due to the invasion of the Sassanians. The Sassanian king Shāpur I (241-272 A.D.) is said to have subjugated the Kuṣāṇas. According to the latest theory on the subject, his invasion, which coincides more or less with the end of the reign of Vāsudeva, is placed some time between 241 and 250 A.D.; consequently, the accession of Kaniṣka, hundred years before this, is placed about 142 A.D.[25] Ghirshman has suggested the accession of Kaniṣka in 144 A.D. on the basis of the material, found in his excavations at Begram.[26] Marshall also accepts the date of the Kuṣāṇas in the second century A.D. as revealed by his excavations at Taxila. In the light of these, the numismatic conclusions adduced above are very valuable; and the problem of the date of Kaniṣka, should be examined afresh.

If the numismatic evidences are not conclusive on the point; and the old view of the date of 78 A.D. is adhered to, we must account for the presence of Kuṣāṇa coins in a territory which was not theirs during their regime and the circumstances of their currency in a period in which the Kuṣāṇas ceased to exist. This would be an unusual phenomenon; but it should not cause any surprise, as it can well be explained. The cause of this unusual phenomenon may be the economic need of the post-Kuṣāṇa period.

The Gupta copper coins are extremely rare, and their silver coins were confined to Western and Central India, and that too came into vogue towards the end of the fourth century A.D. in the time of Candragupta II. The use of punch-marked coins had gone out of vogue long back. Kuṣāṇas too had not issued silver coins. The gold coins of the Guptas could not have met the needs of the middle and lower class people, who required small currencies for meeting their daily needs. We know little about the political conditions of Bihar for centuries before the rise of the Guptas and of eastern U.P. after the fall of the Mitras of Ayodhyā. Therefore, it is very probable that people used the Kuṣāṇa copper coins, which was current in the neighbouring areas of Kānyakubja and Mathura, in absence of their own coinage during the second and third centuries and even after that. In all probability, when the people felt shortage of their own coins, these coins might have infiltrated by way of trade and spread to Bihar and Orissa, far away, outside their original area of currency. There they remained in use for a long time.

When these coins could not meet the demands, it seems, their imitations were issued at places. Among such imitations, the Purī-Kuṣāṇa coins are well-known, as they have been found in abundance in Orissa and Bihar. Even at Mathura imitations were issued having Kuṣāṇa figure of the king on the obverse and parallel lines on the reverse. Recently I had an occasion to see a big lot of such coins with an antiquity dealer at Mathura. Another type of Kuṣāṇa imitation from Kauśāmbī is published by Altekar, with the conjecture that it was the issue of some local Kuṣāṇa governor.[27] That the Kuṣāṇa coins were current outside their territory and long after the extinction of their empire is borne out by the fact that not only coins of Vima Kadphises,

Kaniṣka, Huviṣka and Vāsudeva are found in this area, but the coins of later Kuṣāṇas of the Punjab with Ardokṣo seated on the reverse are also known in this area, though they are not numerous. I had an occasion to see such coins in Vārāṇasī market and obtained a few for my collection.

One may pertinently argue against this suggestion that if the Kuṣāṇa coins went by way of trade in this area, why did they not do so in Madhya Pradesh and Maharashtra? Broach should have got a lot of them. Why did not Indo-Greek and Indo-Scythian coins came in Bihar by way of trade? But these questions are not difficult to answer. If we look to our own times, we shall see that Gwalior coins are current as far as Mathura in one side and Itarsi in the other; but we do not find Hyderabad currency outside its own area. If this is so in an age when time and distance have no consideration, it would have been more so in the ill-equipped ancient days. So, it should be no wonder if Kuṣāṇa coins are not known in Madhya Pradesh and Maharashtra or Indo-Greek and Indo-Scythian coins in Bihar.

However, Kuṣāṇa coins are not quite unknown from Maharashtra-Gujarat area. S.C. Upadhyaya of the Victoria & Albert Museum, Bombay had procured coins of Kaniṣka, Huviṣka and Vāsudeva from that area. One Vima Kadphises coin was found in Karvan in Gujarat.[28] Unfortunately we do not possess detailed informations of the finds of the coins. Many of the hoards that are found, never come to the notice of the scholars and go direct to the melting pot. It is not unlikely that more instances of Kuṣāṇa coins from Western Coast may come to light, if they are properly investigated.

Only in the time of shortage and necessity the import of coinage from another territory is possible. The Kṣatrapas and the Guptas had issued their silver coins in Central and Western India and the Sātavāhana and the local copper coins were in continued currency from the early times and were sufficient to meet their need. So quite naturally they did not require foreign currency. It is not surprising therefore, if Kuṣāṇa coins are not found there in abundance, though sporadic finds are not unknown. Similarly,

Indo-Greek and Indo-Scythian coins were current in a period when the country was flooded with punch-marked coins. There was hardly any necessity for Bihar to import a foreign currency. Had there been any stringency in Bihar, even then it would not have had the Indo-Greek and Indo-Scythian coins from the Punjab, which was far away from Bihar. Maharashtra and Madhya Pradesh were also at a long distance from Kuṣāṇa territory, they too could not have had the Kuṣāṇa coins. It is only from the neighbouring territories, people import coins in the time of need.

There is every possibility that the wide distribution of the Kuṣāṇa coins in the east was the result of the economic needs of the people in the post-Kuṣāṇa period and their presence there is not an indicative of any political expansion of the Kuṣāṇas east-ward beyond Kānyakubja.

References

1. *J.N.S.I.*, XII, p. 122.
2. *I.H.Q.*, XVII, pp. 294-303.
3. *E.I.*, XXI, p. 211.
4. *Op. cit.*, p. 294, f. n. 4.
5. *E.I.*, VIII, p. 181f.
6. See, infra, pp. 55-64
7. For the details of the coins, cf. *J.N.S.I.*, IV, V, VIII & XIV; *BMC., Al.*, intro. p. xciv; pp. 148-58; *A.S.R.*, X. The name of Śivamitra is mentioned in an inscription (*A.S.I.A.R.*, 1913-14, pp. 262-63).
8. *Cf. B.M.C.,A.I.*, intro. p. cxvi; pp. 192-204; *J.N.S.I.*, II, IV & V; *I.M.C.* I; *J.A.S.B.*, XLIX, p. 21.
9. *Cf. B.M.C.,A.I.*, intro. p. lxxxvii, pp. 129-39; *J.N.S.I.*, VIII.
10. *A.S.I.,A.R.*, 1924-25, p. 130.
11. *Ibid.*, p. 132.
12. *J.N.S.I.*, II, p. 124.
13. *Ancient India*, No. 5, p. 97.
14. *B.M.C.,A.I.*, intro. p. cxxii. But R. D. Banerji thought that the inscribed Purī-Kuṣāṇa coins were issued possibly in the sixth century A. D. (*J.B.O.R.S.*, V, pp. 83-84).

15. *Op. cit.*, p. 98.
16. *J.N.S.I.*, XIII, pp. 144-47.
17. *Ibid.*, XII, p. 121.
18. *Ibid.*, pp. 122-23.
19. *Op. cit.*, p. 97.
20. *A.S.I.,A.R.*, 1908-09, p. 35.
21. *J.N.S.I.*, XII, p. 162.
22. *Ibid.*, XII, p. 123.
23. *The Vākāṭaka-Gupta Age*, p. 41. f.n. 2.
24. This view is no more held valid. See infra, pp. 55ff.
25. Majumdar, R.C., *Ancient India*, p. 129.
26. Begram, *Researches archeologiques et historique sur les Kochans.*, pp. 109-84.
27. *J.N.S.I.*, VIII, p. 10.
28. *Ibid.*, XIII, p. 221.

2

Date of Kuṣāṇa Currency in the Eastern India*

A. S. Altekar published a hoard of Kuṣāṇa coins from Buxar, and on the basis of its evidence, he suggested that Magadha was conquered by the Kuṣāṇas early in their dynastic history.[1] A. C. Banerji, in support of his suggestion, compiled a long list of the finds of the Kuṣāṇa coins in eastern India and supplemented it with a list of epigraphical material and art relics of Kuṣāṇa period known in this area.[2] He suggests that U.P., Bihar and possibly the Gangetic delta in Bengal, as well as Orissa, were included for a time within the empire of Kaniṣka.

According to the axiom of the Indian numismatics, copper coins do not generally travel much outside the territory of their circulation; *prima facie* there appears some justification for the conclusions drawn by these scholars. Since the suggestions are of far reaching consequences in the reconstruction of the history and no other sources are known to support them, they require a fair, careful, balanced and unbiased study. I propose to examine them critically.

Banerji has given the following list of the coins found in the Bengal:

(i) A copper coin of Kaniṣka, found in 1882 at Tāmluk in the Midnapur district.

---

* Originally published in *Journal of the Numismatic Society of India*, XV.ii (1953), pp. 178-184.

(ii) A base metal coin of Vāsudeva found in Murshidabad district.

(iii) A gold coin of Vāsudeva, found in 1909 in Bogra district.

(iv) Three Kuṣāṇa coins from North Bengal. Two of them came from Mahāsthān and one of them belonged to Vāsudeva and the other is not assigned to any particular king. The third coin came from Malda and belonged to Vāsudeva. (Banerji has mentioned these coins as silver pieces. But no silver coin of this dynasty is ever known from this area. The silver coins of the Kuṣāṇas known elsewhere are, in all likelihood, forgeries).[3]

Of the four entries in the above list, three refer to non-copper coinage belonging to Vāsudeva. Gold and silver coins may travel far from their place of origin by way of trade. So one can well suggest that they came to Bengal by way of commerce. Moreover, hardly any scholar thinks of Vāsudeva's dominion in this part of the country. So, we have only a single copper piece of Kaniṣka, which was found at Tāmluk, the ancient port of international importance. It seems idle to talk of the Kuṣāṇa rule in Bengal for even a short period, on the basis of this single coin.

Next is the list of finds from Orissa given by Banerji:

(i) Copper coins of Kaniṣka and Huviṣka were found at Bhañjikā in Mayurabhanj district. (This hoard was found in 1923 and included the coins of Purī-Kuṣāṇa type, of which some were inscribed.[4])

(ii) 112 copper coins of Great Kuṣāṇas were found at Mayurabhanj by R. D. Banerji. (This hoard also, was found in 1923 or 1924, but the find spot is not recorded. The hoard also included 170 Purī-Kuṣāṇa coins.[5])

(iii) Kuṣāṇa coins were found in the excavations at Virāṭgarh in Mayurabhanj district. (P. Acharya states that a few Kuṣāṇa coins were found with a large number of Purī-Kuṣāṇa coins in this excavation.[6])

(iv) Copper coins of Kaniṣka and Huviṣka were found at Śiśupālagarh. (Only one coin each of the two kings were found in the excavations, with the four coins of Purī-Kuṣāṇas. These coins have been found in the upper level which may be dated according to the excavation report to 200-350 A.D.[7])

The information given within brackets is added by me and was not disclosed by Banerji. They show that Kuṣāṇa coins were not found in Orissa independent of Purī-Kuṣāṇa coins. The Bhañjikā hoard had the inscribed coins which have the legend in the characters of the fourth century A.D.[8] It is thus clear that coins were not deposited earlier than that period. The excavation report of Śiśupālagarh informs us that the Kaniṣka coin was found on the late unstratified layer and the coin of Huviṣka, which was in a fair condition, was found in the upper level of the period IIB, i.e., dating towards the end of second century A.D.[9]

This shows that the Kuṣāṇa coins were current in Orissa in the period, when the Kuṣāṇa empire had ceased to exist in northern India. So, there arises no question of their domination over this area.

Banerji records three finds from Bihar:

(i) A gold coin of Huviṣka was found in Belwadaga thana and a copper coin of Kaniṣka in the Karra thana of the Ranchi district.

(ii) Excavations at Pāṭaliputra yielded two copper coins of Kaniṣka and more of Vima Kadphises and Huviṣka. (Altekar has recently published the list of the coins which were found in the Kumrahāra and Bulandībāgh excavations near Patna in 1912-13. He gives the list of the coins as Vima Kadphises 3, Kaniṣka 12, Huviṣka 30.[10])

(iii) Kuṣāṇa coins have been found at Vaiśālī in large number.

To this list should be added the Buxar hoard, which Altekar has published, suggesting the Kuṣāṇa occupation of Magadha.

(iv) Buxar hoard of copper coins included 23 of Vima

Kadphises, 159 of Kaniṣka, 172 of Huviṣka, 38 undecipherable and 10 Ayodhyā (Kosala) coins of Bull-and-Cock series.[11]

One more find from this area is known to me.

(v) Ganesh Chaube of Bangari, district Champaran, sent me in 1952 a few copper coins of Kuṣāṇas collected from his area. They included a coin of Vima Kadphises and the rest were of Huviṣka.

Of these finds, the coins found in the excavations at Pāṭaliputra and Vaiśālī would have been the best evidence, had their stratification been properly recorded. Altekar has pointed out that square and round cast coins were found in large number in Kumrahāra excavations. He concludes that this tends to show that the copper currency of the Kuṣāṇas succeeded in completely ousting the indigenous copper currency of cast coins. This, he says, took place in 75 A.D.[12] But in absence of stratification there is hardly any justification for suggesting such a hypothesis. As pointed out above the Śiśupālagarh excavations give the date of the currency of the Kuṣāṇa coins at about 200 A.D. There too, cast coins were found and they suggest that they were in currency from 50 A.D. to 350 A.D. Three of the coins, out of a total nine, were found in the upper layer of period IIA attributable to *c.* A.D. 50-100; the same number were found in the early level of period IIB, datable at *c.* A.D. 100-125 and the remaining were obtained from later deposits which may be assigned to *c.* 200-350 A.D.[13] The coin of Huviṣka, here was found in the upper level of period IIB, datable to *circa* 200 A.D. That the cast coins had continued to be current in the second-third century A.D. is also borne out from a hoard recently found in the vicinity of Kauśāmbī by the veteran coin-collector Braj Mohan Vyas. It includes seven square cast coins along with more than a thousand coins of Maghas,[14] who are known to have ruled in Kauśāmbī in second-third century A.D. It is therefore not unlikely that like Śiśupālagarh and Kauśāmbī the cast coins had continued to be current in Magadha too in the second and third centuries A.D. The Kusāṇa coins might have followed them just they did in Orissa. However, in absence of any definite knowledge about the level of their finds, we should not attach any importance to the coins found in the excavations at Pāṭaliputra and Vaiśālī for determining the period of their currency.

The Buxar hoard should be assessed on its merit of being an intact hoard. Before doing so, I would enlist the hoards that are known from eastern U.P. Banerji has failed to give any such list. His list contained two notices of Kuṣāṇa coins from Basti district, which were picks from various sites and serve no purpose, other than showing that they were current in that locality. But following hoards are known to me from this area:

(i) 105 copper Kuṣāṇa coins were found at Sahet-Mahet in the cell of a monastery in the excavations of 1908-09. It included 2 coins of Kaniṣka, 2 of Huviṣka, 96 of Vāsudeva and the remaining were badly effaced.[15]

(ii) 100 copper Kuṣāṇa coins were found in the village Bindwal in Azamgarh district in 1949-50 and the kings represented there were Kaniṣka and Huviṣka.[16]

(iii) A hoard of Kuṣāṇa copper coins was found on the bank of a *nālā* in the village Nai in Azamgarh district in about 1938. A few coins of this hoard were shown to me by a resident of that village, which suggested that the hoard included the coins of Kaniṣka, Huviṣka and the Cock-Bull type of Ayodhyā.

(iv) A big hoard of several hundred copper Kuṣāṇa coins was found at Sidhārī, on the outskirt of Azamgarh town in about 1950, when a foundation trench was being dug for a house. A portion of it formed part of the collection of Ramashanker Rawat of Azamgarh. Most of the coins were of Kaniṣka and Huviṣka; and the Bull-Cock type coins of Ayodhyā.

Of the five finds listed above, at least three have a common feature that Kuṣāṇa coins were associated with Ayodhyā coins of Bull-Cock type. Ayodhyā coins are comparatively few in all these hoards. According to the axiom of the numismatics, the Ayodhyā coins were either issued earlier than the Kuṣāṇa coins or after them. Altekar is of opinion that the Mitra kings of Ayodhyā (who issued the Cock-Bull type coins) were most probably slightly later than the time of Kaniṣka and Vāsudeva.[17] He places them in the second century A.D. and suggest that they probably ruled as the feudatories of the Kuṣāṇas and were allowed to issue coins. This suggestion needs close scrutiny.

India knows three big empires, during the historical period of 2500 years, viz. Nanda-Maurya, Gupta and Mughal. The coinage of Nanda-Maurya period, i.e., the Punch-marked coinage, is still an enigma, but we know about the coins of the two other empires. Not a single instance is known where the rulers of these empires had allowed their feudatories to issue their own coinage. The later Mughals, during the period of the decadence of their empire, had no doubt tolerated the minting of the coins by their feudatories; but even those feudatories did not dare to issue coins in their own name. Altekar, himself has admitted that no Gupta feudatory was ever permitted to mint any coins.[18] I wonder then how he thinks that Kuṣāṇas would have permitted a feudatory family, ruling at Ayodhyā, to issue its own coinage? Even if we presume that they did permit the minting to their Ayodhyā feudatories, how is it that we do not find any Kuṣāṇa influence over those coins? If the Ayodhyā feudatories issued their own coins, side by side of the imperial coinage, it should be expected that their coins should have been more in currency in Ayodhyā kingdom, being the local currency than that of the Kuṣāṇas. In our own times, we had many princely states, under the British rule, who were issuing their own coins within their territories. They can well be cited in analogy to the situation in Ayodhyā under the Kuṣāṇas. Hyderabad and Gwalior were the two principal states who were issuing their own coins. Their coins were found current along with the British currency in their territories; but they always remained more numerous there than the British currency. The same way, the Ayodhyā coins should have been more numerous than the Kuṣāṇas in the above hoards found in Azamgarh district, situated near the heart of the kingdom. But it was not so. The suggestion of Kuṣāṇa domination over Ayodhyā during the reign of Mitra kings is only imaginary.

It may be assumed that Mitra kings of Ayodhyā were formerly feudatories to Kuṣāṇas and during that period they did not issue their own coins; with the decadence of the Kuṣāṇa empire they became independent and issued their own coins. This would account the constitution of the hoards. But we have nothing to show that Mitra coins could be dated in the period after the Kuṣāṇas. They cannot in any case be placed later than second century A.D.

There is nothing for the present to suggest the contemporaneity or posteriority of the Mitra kings of Ayodhyā with the Kuṣāṇa kings. The natural conclusion, from the Buxar and Sahet-Mahet hoards, would be that the Mitra coins were followed in this area by the Kuṣāṇa coins earliest towards the end of the second century A.D.

Evidently, it is highly improbable that the Kuṣāṇa coins would have come into currency in the eastern U.P., Bihar and Orissa, before the end of the second century A.D.

The date of the rise of the Kuṣāṇas or for the matter of that, of Kaniṣka, is a most vexed problem of Indian chronology. Most of the scholars place his accession in 78 A.D. If that date is accepted it may be said with certainty that by 178 A.D. the great empire of Kaniṣka had passed away, for the four kings of his dynasty did not rule for more than hundred years. If there was no trace of the Kuṣāṇas by the end of second century A.D. The currency of their coins in the period when they had ceased to exist and that too in a territory, of the domination over which, we have no evidence, is an unusual phenomenon and needs some valid explanation.

The unusual phenomenon is explained if economic need for the post-Kuṣāṇa period is taken into account. Gupta copper coins are extremely rare, and their silver coins were confined to

Western India and Madhyadeśa and that too from the end of the fourth century A.D. in the time of Candragupta II. The use of Punch-marked coins had gone out of vogue long time back. Kuṣāṇas, themselves had not issued silver coins. The gold coins of the Guptas could not have met the day-to-day needs of the middle and lower class of people. They needed small currencies to meet their daily needs. Little is known about the political conditions of Bihar for the three centuries before the rise of the Guptas and of the eastern U.P. after fall of the Mitras of Ayodhyā. It is, very probable that people used the Kuṣāṇa copper coins, that were current in the neighbouring areas of Kānyakubja and Mathura, in the absence or shortage of their own coinage during the third century and even later, when the people felt shortage of their own coins, these coins infiltrated by way of trade and spread outside their own area into Bihar and Orissa. There they remained in use for long.

When these coins could not meet their demands, their imitations were issued at places. Among such imitations Purī-Kuṣāṇa coins are well-known; they have been found in abundance in Orissa and Bihar. Even at Mathura imitations were issued having Kuṣāṇa figure of the king. I had an occassion to see a big lot of such coins with an antiquity dealer at Mathura. Another type of Kuṣāṇa imitation is published by Altekar, as the issue of local Kuṣāṇa governor.[19] The Kuṣāṇa coins were current outside their territory and long after the extinction of their empire is borne out by the fact that not only the coins of Vima Kadaphises, Kaniṣka, Huviṣka and Vāsudeva are found in this area, but the coins of later Kuṣāṇas of the Punjab with Ardokṣo seated on the reverse, are also known in this area. Such coins are occasionally seen in the Vārāṇasī.

It may well be argued that if Kuṣāṇa coins went to this area by way of trade, why did they not do so to Madhya Pradesh, Maharastra and Gujarat? Broach should have had them predominantly. Why did not Indo-Greek and Indo-Scythian coins came in Bihar by way of trade? It is not difficult to answer these questions. In the recent past Gwalior coins are current as far as

Mathura on one side and Itarsi on the other; but we do not find Hyderabad currency outside its own area. If this was so, when time and distance had no consideration, it would have been more so in the ill-equipped ancient days.

It should be no wonder if Kuṣāṇa coins are not known in Madhya Pradesh, Maharashtra and Gujarat or Indo-Greek and Indo-Scythian coins are not known in Bihar. Kuṣāṇa coins are not so unknown in Gujarat. S.C. Upadhyaya of the Victoria & Albert Museum, Bombay had procured some coins of Kaniṣka, Huviṣka and Vāsudava from that area. One Vima Kadphises coin was found at Karvan in Gujarat.[20] Unfortunately we do not possess detailed informations of such coins finds. Many of the hoards that are found, never come to the notice of the scholars and go direct to the melting pot. It is not unlikely that such instances of Kuṣāṇa coins might come to light, if they are properly investigated.

It is needless to say that only in the times of shortage and necessity the import of coinage from other territory is possible. The Kṣatrapas and the Guptas had issued their silver coins in central and western India; Sātavāhana and earlier local copper coins were in continued currency from the early times. They were sufficient to meet their needs; naturally they did not require foreign currency. It is no suprise if Kuṣāṇa coins are not found there in any appreciable quantity. Similarly, Indo-Greek and Indo-Scythian coins were current in a period when the country was flooded with the punch-marked coins. There was hardly any necessity for Bihar to import a foreign currency. Had there been any stringency, even then it would not have had the Indo-Greek and Indo-Scythian coins from the Punjab, which was far away. It is only from the neighbouring territories that people import coins in time of need.

The wide diffusion of the Kuṣāṇa coins in eastern U.P., Bihar and Orissa might have necessitated to meet the economic needs of the people in the post-Kuṣāṇa period. They are no indication of any political expansion of the Kuṣāṇas eastward beyond Kānyakubja.

References

1. *J.N.S.I.*, XII, p. 121.
2. *Ibid.*, XIII, p. 107; *I.H.Q.*, XXVII, pp. 294-303.
3. *Cf. J.N.S.I.*, XIV, p. 34 ff.
4. *A.S.I., A.R.*, 1924-25, p. 130.
5. *Ibid.*, p. 132.
6. *J.N.S.I.*, II, p. 124.
7. *Ancient India* no 5, p. 97.
8. *B.M.C.,A.I.*, intro. p. cxii. In the opinion of R.D. Banerjee inscribed Purī-Kuṣāṇa coins were issued possibly in the sixth century A.D. (*J.B.O.R.S.*, I. pp. 83-84).
9. *Ancient India*, no 5. p. 98.
10. *J.N.S.I.* XIII, pp. 144-47.
11. *Ibid.*, XII, p. 121.
12. *Ibid.*, pp. 12-23.
13. *Ancient India*, no. 5, p. 97.
14. *J.N.S.I.*, XXVIII, p. 47.
15. *A.S.I., A.R.*, 1908-9, p. 35.
16. *J.N.S.I.*, XI., p. 162.
17. *Ibid.*, XII, p. 123.
18. *The Vākāṭaka-Gupta Age*, p. 41. fn. 2.
19. *J.N.S.I.*, VIII, p. 10.
20. *Ibid.*, XIII, p. 221.

3

Gold Amulets and the Kuṣāṇa History*

WHILE publishing an interesting gold amulet, an imitation of a coin of Kuṣāṇa king Huviṣka, that was found in an excavation at Sadargalli in Patna city, Altekar has again raised the problem of Kuṣāṇa rule in Bihar.[1] Herein he has also mentioned another similar amulet that was found by Cunningham in the last century buried below the *Vajrāsana* throne at Bodh Gaya.[2]

He thinks that the gold Kuṣāṇa currency was so common in Bihar that the ladies there had taken a fancy for some of its types and ordered the goldsmiths to prepare pendants or talismans in their imitation and that this could not have been possible if the coins had come only by commercial intercourse.[3]

The commonness of any particular coin in any particular area does no doubt suggest a domination over that area of the issuer of that coin. But this conclusion is not true in many cases. We have instances where coins coming from outside the country by the way of trade were fairly common in this country. And owing to their fascination for them, people had begun to use them as pendants or make their imitations in metal and clay for that purpose.

The Roman coins are known in abundance in the south-western part of this country where they were current towards the beginning of the Christian era. But the Romans did never enter this land even for a moment as rulers. Yet, the Roman coins

* Originally published in *Journal of the Numismatic Society of India*, XXI.ii (1959), pp. 188-193.

had found favour with the people of the country and they had prepared metal and clay imitations having two holes, same as is the case on these two Kuṣāṇa imitations.

At Nāgārjunīkoṇḍā, in *Stupa* no. 6, among the relics were found two tiny gold coin-like medallions, too thin to have been used as coins. Each one had two holes at the top showing that they were used as pendants. One bears the portrait of a woman and the other of a young man; both show marked Roman influence.[4]

Such imitation of Roman coins in clay are known from many sites in India, viz. Śiśupālgarh,[5] Rājghāt (Vārāṇasī),[6] Kauśāmbī.[7] Garh (near Ujjain),[8] Karāḍ (district Satara),[9] Brahmapurī (Kolhapur),[10] Koṇḍāpur,[11] Candrāvalli, (Mysore).[12] At some of these places Roman coins were not current.

Similarly the Venecian ducates or sequins, that came to India by way of trade in the fourteenth century A.D., were imitated by the people for the same purpose. India-made dies for making these imitations were found in the Kaira district of Gujarat.[13] An interesting imitation in gold is in Madras Museum.[14] The Prince of Wales Museum possesses about a dozen brass imitations with loops. As late as 1882 at Bombay the imitations of sequins were common for ornamental purposes; a large part of women of the lower and middle classes wore them round their necks. They were made in large quantity, but the quality was usually poor.[15]

These instances are just parallel to the Kuṣāṇa amulets. I do not know what Altekar would conclude from these Roman and Venecian ducates and their imitations. It is very much apparant that they weaken the arguments for the suggestion of the Kuṣāṇa rule in Bihar.

The finds of the Kuṣāṇa pendants at Patna and Bodha Gaya themselves point out that Kuṣāṇa gold coins were scarce in that region, which could never have been the case, had Bihar been under the Kuṣāṇa domination. They had their reach only among a few rich people, and that too in such a limited number that they could not use the coins as pendants, as we find in the case of the Roman coins. It was the rarity or scarcity of these coins that fascinated the people. It is well-known that rarity of a thing attracts the rich.

References

1. *J.N.S.I.*, XX, pp. 1-3.
2. Cunningham, *Mahābodhi*, pl. XXV, 17.
3. *Op. cit.*, p. 3.
4. *Buddhist Antiquities of Nāgārjunīkoṇḍā*, p. 21-22.
5. *Ancient India*, No. 5, p. 101, pl. LB.
6. *J.N.S.I.*, III, p. 77, pl. V. 17-19.
7. Unpublished; in Allahabad Museum.
8. *Report of the Archaeological Department, Gwalior State*, 1938-39, pl. 18, pl. XXVIII b.
9. *Explorations at Karāḍ*, p. 30, pl. XIII c.d.
10. *Excavations at Brahmapuri*, 1945-46, Pl. XXVI B, 6.
11. *A.B.O.R.I.*, XXII, pp. 179-80, pl. XIIIb.
12. *Supplement to Annual Report of the Mysore Archaeological Department* 1929, p. 29.
13. *I.A.*, II, p. 213.
14. *Catalogue of Venecian Coins in the Madras Government Museum*, pp. 4-5.
15. *Ibid.*, p. 4.

4

Date of Kaniṣka*

THE period of the Kuṣāṇas lies somewhere between the decline of the great Mauryan empire and the rise of the other great empire of the Guptas.

The Mauryan empire collapsed after the *coup d'état* of Puṣyamitra Śuṅga, in *c.* 184 B.C. It is not unlikely that the empire began to crumble much earlier, though not immediately after the death of Aśoka, which occurred in *c.* 232 B.C. It seems to me that most of the Mauryan provinces became independent with the advent of the Greeks of Bactria across the north-western gate of the empire in the reign of the Mauryan king Śāliśuka in *c.* 208 or 204 B.C. But for the purpose of the present discussion, an earlier date, *c.* 215 B.C. may be acceptable.

The expansion of the Gupta empire began with the successful expedition of Samudragupta, which is placed with all reliance in *c.* A.D. 350.

Our main problem is to put the 100 years of the reign of the Kuṣāṇas at the proper place in a political chronology within the period of 565 years that elapsed between the fall of the Mauryas (i.e., *c.* 215 B.C.) and the rise of the Guptas (i.e., A.D. 350). Once we are able to build up a political chronology of this period and fix in it properly the reign of the Kuṣāṇas, it would not be difficult to determine the epoch of the Kaniṣka era.

---

* Originally submitted to the Colloquium on the Date of Kaniska organised at the School of Oriental and African Studies, University of London in 1960. *Papers on the Date of Kaniska* (Ed. A.L. Basham), Leiden, 1968, pp. 114-120.

The coins that have been found at various sites that fall within the heart of the Kuṣāṇa kingdom show that four powerful states rose up from the ruins of the Mauryan empire at Mathura, Kauśāmbī, Ayodhyā and Ahicchatrā. They also show that they had a long and peaceful rule. So the Kuṣāṇas can be placed in the political chronology of these territories, only after the fall of those local dynasties. It is quite possible that the Kuṣāṇas were instrumental in their fall. But so far no attention has been given to the history of these post-Mauryan kingdoms of the Gangetic plains.

Mathura was the stronghold of Kaniṣka and his successors. So I shall look to it first. The coins of the local rulers that have been found there and in its vicinity reveal that the kingdom that rose at Mathura, after the fall of the Mauryan empire, had no less than twenty rulers: Gomitra,[1] Sūryamitra,[2] Brahmamitra,[3] Dhruvamitra,[4] Dṛḍhamitra,[5] Viṣṇumitra,[6] Śeṣadatta,[7] Puruṣadatta,[8] Uttamadatta,[9] Rāmadatta,[10] Kāmadatta,[11] Bhavadatta,[12] Balabhūti,[13] Mahākṣatrapa Rājuvula,[14] Mahākṣatrapa Śoḍāsa,[15] Kṣatrapa Toraṇaḍāsa,[16] Kṣatrapa Hagāna,[17] Kṣatrapa Hagāmaṣa,[18] Kṣatrapa Śivadatta[19] and Kṣatrapa Śivaghoṣa.[20]

We need not go here into the details of the chronology of these rulers; it would be enough to say that all the coins have a close affinity. Even the coins of Mahākṣatrapa Rājuvula and his successors follow the coin-type of the Datta rulers. This shows a continuous rule for these twenty rulers in succession without any break. If we assume a period of eighteen years for each ruler,[21] these twenty rulers would have ruled for about 360 years before the Kuṣāṇas or any other rulers stepped in at Mathura.

The palaeography of the coins of Gomitra shows that they were the earliest issue of the kingdom and were issued towards the end of the third century B.C. If the kingdom of Mathura came into existence in *c.* 215 B.C., immediately after the fall of the Mauryan empire, then these rulers ruled at least up to A.D. 145; and only after them the Kuṣāṇas would have come to Mathura, at the earliest.

At Kauśāmbī, the capital of ancient Vatsa, a few Buddha images have been found bearing inscriptions dated in the early years of Kaniṣka. These inscriptions are taken to be an indication of Kuṣāṇa rule over that country. Excavations are being carried out at this ancient site. The details of these excavations are not yet available; but a brief note by the excavator, for the season 1949-50, is before us.[22] According to it, the lower strata (4-7) contained the coins of local rulers, whose names ended with Mitra. In stratum 3 and subsequent strata were found the coins of another local dynasty, whose names ended with Magha. Along with the Magha coins, Kuṣāṇa coins were found in stratum 3. They seem to be confined to this stratum. So we may conveniently infer from these data that the Kuṣāṇa coins entered Kauśāmbī only after the Mitra rule had ceased and the Maghas had begun their rule. But the Kuṣāṇa coins are in no way indicative of the Kuṣāṇa occupation of the country, for the simple reason that Magha coins continue in subsequent strata, where the Kuṣāṇa coins are conspicuous by their absence. These Kuṣāṇa coins may be drifts. However, they are valuable for the dating of the Kuṣāṇas.

The coins of no less than nineteen Mitra rulers of the pre-Magha period have been found at Kauśāmbī. They are: Vavaghoṣa,[23] Aśvaghoṣa,[24] Parvata,[25] Indradeva,[26] Sudeva,[27] Mitra,[28] Rādhamitra,[29] Agnimitra,[30] Jyeṣṭhamitra,[31] Bṛhaspatimitra,[32] Suramitra,[33] Varuṇamitra,[34] Poṭhamitra,[35] Sarpamitra,[36] Prajāpatimitra,[37] Satyamitra,[38] Rājamitra,[39] Rajanīmitra,[40] and Devamitra.[41]

Another ruler Śivamitra is known from his inscription found at Kauśāmbī.[42] These twenty rulers would have ruled for about 360 years.

Palaeographically, the coins of Vavaghoṣa and Aśvaghoṣa are the earliest and may be placed in the latter part of the third century B.C. If they rose immediately after the Mauryas in 215 B.C., then the twenty rulers ruled till A.D. 145 and thereafter the Maghas followed them. This means that the stratum 3, where the Kuṣāṇa coins have been found, should be dated later than A.D. 145.

If we look at the excavation-finds from the other end, the coins of Gaṇendra, i.e., Gaṇapati Nāga were found immediately above the coins of the Maghas in the stratum 1. The Magha rulers so far known are eleven: Bhadramagha,[43] Vaiśravaṇa,[44] Śivamagha,[45] Satamagha,[46] Vijayamagha,[47] Puramagha,[48] Yugamagha,[49] Bhīmavarman,[50] Nāvika,[51] Puṣvaśrī,[52] and Dhanadeva.[53] These ruled for about 198 years. Gaṇapati Nāga was one of the rulers who was subdued by Samudragupta during his expedition in A.D 350. As such, the Magha rule might have begun in *c.* A.D. 152, nearly the same date as we reached earlier. The Kuṣāṇa coins at Kauśāmbī may therefore be dated only in *c.* A.D. 145-152.

As at Kauśāmbī, a Buddha image dated in the early years of Kaniṣka was found at Śrāvastī. This appears to suggest Kuṣāṇa influence over the Kosala area. Several hoards of copper coins have been found in Kosala as well as in the neighbouring territories; these include the coins of the local rulers of Ayodhyā along with those of the Kuṣāṇas. In these hoards, the Kosala coins are always few in number and suggest that the Kuṣāṇas followed the local rulers of Kosala in the latter's territory.[54]

The coins of the local rulers that have been found at Ayodhyā belong to the following fifteen rulers: Mūladeva,[55] Vāyudeva,[56] Viśākhadeva,[57] Dhanadeva,[58] Pāthadeva (?),[59] Śivadatta,[60] Naradatta,[61] Jyeṣṭhadatta,[62] Kumudasena,[63] Ajavarman,[64] Saṅghamitra,[65] Vijayamitra,[66] Satyamitra,[67] Devamitra,[68] and Āryamitra.[69]

In an inscription, found at Ayodhyā, we find mention of king Dhanadeva (in all probability the same as is known from the coins) the son of Phalgudeva, who claims to be the 'sixth' from the *senāpati* Puṣyamitra, the king of Ayodhyā, and the performer of two *aśvamedhas.*[70] The title *senāpati* was borne by Puṣyamitra Śuṅga and his *aśvamedhas* are well-known from the *Mahābhāṣya* and the *Mālavikāgnimitra*. So the inscription undoubtedly refers to Puṣyamitra Śuṅga. Since Dhanadeva's name does not appear in the *Purāṇic* list of Śuṅgas it appears that he was only some collateral scion of the dynasty. If the word 'sixth' in the inscription meant 'sixth generation', we may take it that five generations before Dhanadeva his family had some relations with the Śuṅgas. Incidentally, the *Harṣacarita* informs that one Mūladeva (who may be Mūladeva of the coins) killed Sumitra (Vasumitra) the son of Agnimitra. All these facts taken together suggest that the Śuṅga territory of Ayodhyā was usurped by Mūladeva in *c.* 130 B.C.

Now from *c.* 130 B.C. onwards sixteen rulers of Ayodhyā, including Phalgudeva whose coins are not known, ruled for 188 years, i.e., up to *c.* A.D. 158. The Kuṣāṇas would have come only later than this date at Kosala.

Another kingdom, that of Pañcāla, with its capital at Ahicchatrā, rose after the Mauryas, and had no less than 21 rulers who are known from their coins, which are all uniform in pattern and show no break. They are: Rudragupta,[71] Jayagupta,[72] Dāmagupta,[73] Vaṅgapāla,[74] Viśvapāla,[75] Yajñapāla,[76] Vasusena,[77] Sūryamitra,[78] Viṣṇumitra,[79] Dhruvamitra,[80] Indramitra,[81] Agnimitra,[82] Bhānumitra,[83] Bhūmimitra,[84] Jayamitra,[85] Phālgunīmitra,[86] Bṛhaspatimitra,[87] Aṇumitra,[88] Āyumitra,[89] Varuṇamitra,[90] and Prajāpatimitra.[91]

Though palaeographically none of the coins seems to be earlier than 200 B.C., it seems safe to assume the rise of the dynasty a little earlier, in 215 B.C., the date assumed above for the decline of the Mauryas. As such these rulers ruled for about 378 years, i.e., up to *c.* A.D. 163.

Excavations were conducted at Ahicchatrā in 1940-44; but no report is available. However, from an article on the pottery found in the excavations, we know that in the lower strata VIII and VII square and round cast coins were found. The coins of the local rulers were found in strata VI and V and they were followed by Kuṣāṇa and imitation Kuṣāṇa coins in stratum IV; and in the earliest layer of stratum III were found the coins of Acyuta, who was defeated by Samudragupta in *c.* A.D. 350.[92] These data make it clear that the Mitras were followed by the Kuṣāṇas; and the latter would have appeared on the scene in *c.* A.D. 163 at the earliest.

If the excavation data are examined from the upper period downwards, the date A.D. 350 is fixed for Acyuta. Before him are the Kuṣāṇa and imitation Kuṣāṇa coins. It is generally believed that the imitation Kuṣāṇa coins were popular issues in India for about a century after the Kuṣāṇas. This means that Kuṣāṇa and imitation Kuṣāṇa coins taken together covered a period of about 200 years before A.D. 350. This shows that Kuṣāṇa coins might have appeared a little earlier than A.D. 163, in about 150.

We have thus the approximate dates A.D. 145 (from Mathura), 145-152 (from Kauśāmbī), 158 (from Ayodhyā) and 150-163 (from Ahichatrā), when the Kuṣāṇas seem to have entered into the Gaṅgā-Yamunā valley. These dates do not present us with any precise date for the epoch of the Kuṣāṇa rule; but they make it amply clear that the Kuṣāṇas cannot be dated earlier than the middle of the second century A.D. We should now look in the light of these facts for the exact date of the beginning of Kaniṣka's reign.

It is not proposed to take up that question here; but it may be pointed out that the date A.D. 144 suggested by Ghirshman[93] is very near to our conclusions. If the arguments adduced in favour of this date from the archaeology of Afghanistan and Central Asia are not weighty enough in themselves, the present conclusions based on numismatics offer strong support to it from the Indian side.

References

1. *B.M.C.,A.I.*, p. 169.
2. *Ibid.*, p. 174.
3. *Ibid.*, p. 173.
4. *Excavations at Rairh*, p. 68.
5. *B.M.C.,A.I.*, p. 174.
6. *Ibid.*, p. 175.
7. *Ibid.*, p. 174; intro., p. cx.
8. *Ibid.*, p. 176.
9. *Ibid.*, p. 177.

10. *Ibid.*, p. 179.
11. *Ibid.*, p. 182.
12. *I.M.C.*, p. 193; *B.M.C.,A.I.*, intro. p. cxi.
13. *B.M.C.,A.I.*, p. 178.
14. *Ibid.*, p. 185.
15. *Ibid.*, p. 190.
16. *Ibid.*, intro. p. cxii.
17. Unpublished, in the cabinet of the Prince of Wales Museum, Bombay. His coins, issued jointly with Hagāmaṣa are well-known (*B.M.C.,A.I.*, p. 184).
18. *B.M.C.*,A.I., p. 183.
19. *Ibid.*, p. 183.
20. *Ibid.*, intro., p. cxii.
21. The average of the generations of various dynasties of India in the historical period varies from 21 to 31 years. Only one or two dynasties are known to have had generations averaging a little less than 20 years. A still lower average of 18 years has been accepted for these calculations.
22. *Annual Bibliography*, 1949-55, pp. xxxvi-xiv.
23. *J.N.S.I.*, IV, pp. 2-4.
24. *B.M.C.,A.I.*, p. 150.
25. *Ibid.*, p. 150.
26. *J.N.S.I.*, XXI, p. 67.
27. *B.M.C.,A.I.*, p. 150.
28. *J.N.S.I.*, VIII, p. 7.
29. *Ibid.*, IV, p. 4.
30. *B.M.C.,A.I.*, p. 153.
31. *Ibid.*, p. 154.
32. *Ibid.*, p. 150.
33. *J.N.S.I.*, IV, p. 5.
34. *Ibid.*, p. 6.
35. *Ibid.*, pp. 133-34.
36. *Ibid.*, p. 135.
37. *Ibid.*, p. 7.
38. *Ibid.*, p. 134.
39. *Ibid.*, p. 8.
40. *Ibid.*, p. 10.
41. *C.A.S.R.*, X, p. 4.

42. *A.S.I.,A.R.*, 1913-14, p. 26.
43. *J.N.S.I.*, II, p. 105.
44. *Ibid.*, p. 106.
45. *Ibid.*, p. 105.
46. *Ibid.*, IV, pp. 10-11.
47. *Ibid.*, pp. 11-12.
48. *Ibid.*, VIII, p. 8.
49. *Ibid.*, p. 9.
50. *Ibid.*, II, p. 108.
51. *Ibid.*, IV, p. 136; VIII, p. 11.
52. *Ibid.*, IV, p. 136.
53. *B.M.C.,A.I.*, p. 153.
54. *I.H.Q.*, XXIX, p. 216.
55. *B.M.C.,A.I.*, p. 130.
56. *Ibid.*, p. 130.
57. *Ibid.*, p. 311.
58. *Ibid.*, p. 132.
59. *Ibid.*, intro., p. lxxxix.
60. *Ibid.*, p. 133.
61. *Ibid.*, p. 134.
62. *J.N.S.I.*, VIII, p. 14.
63. *B.M.C.,A.I.*, p. 137.
64. *I.M.C.*, p. 150.
65. *B.M.C.,A.I.*, p. 138.
66. *Ibid.*, p. 138.
67. *Ibid.*, p. 135.
68. *I.M.C.*, p. 151.
69. *B.M.C.,A.I.*, p. 137.
70. *E.I.*, XX, p. 57.
71. *B.M.C.,A.I.*, p. 192.
72. *Ibid.*, p. 202.
73. *J.N.S.I.*, II, p. 115; XV, p. 43.
74. *Ibid.*, II, p. 115; IV, pp. 19-20.
75. *B.M.C.,A.I.*, p. 192.
76. *J.N.S.I.*, IV, pp. 17-18.

77. *Ibid.,* II, p. 115.
78. *B.M.C.,A.I.,* p. 193.
79. *Ibid.,* p. 202.
80. *Ibid.,* p. 199.
81. *Ibid.,* p. 203.
82. *Ibid.,* p. 199.
83. *Ibid.,* p. 195.
84. *Ibid.,* p. 108.
85. *Ibid.,* p. 203.
86. *Ibid.,* p. 194.
87. *I.M.C.,* p. 185.
88. *J.A.S.B.,* XLIX, p. 21.
89. *Ibid.*
90. *J.N.S.I.,* V, p. 17.
91. *Ibid.,* III, pp. 79-80.
92. *Ancient India,* No. 1, pp. 37-40.
93. Begram, *Researches, archelogiqus et historique Sur les Kochans,* pp. 109-84.

5

Kaniṣka, Son of Huviṣka*

A GERMAN Archaeological mission, under the leadership of H. Härtel, the Director of the Museum of Indian Art, Berlin-Dahlem, excavated an ancient mound at Sonkh, near Govardhan in Mathura district. In the month of February 1973. Härtel invited me to come to his Camp to see the coins that his team has found in the excavated trenches and on the surface around the site. They included many interesting coins. Of them, the most important was a copper coin that was found on surface, a little away from the excavated site. Härtel was very kind to let me have a free choice in its publication.[1] With my sincere thanks to him, I am publishing the coin. It is as follows:

AE; Round: 2 cms in diameter.

Obverse: Within a square incuse (the incuse line on the right and bottom are clear on the coin; the other two sides are off the flan) a male figure standing to front wearing a short tunic, close fitting trousers and boots; a circular halo around the head;[2] he holds a long staff with a triangle-like top (trunkated) in his half raised left hand; right arm is akimbo placed on the hip. Brāhmī legend appears on his right in bold letters written in a straight line (beginning from VIII going up to XI) *Huviṣkasya.*

Reverse: A long tree in a small square railing on the

---

* Originally published in *Journal of the Numismatic Society of India*, XXXV (1973), pp. 123-126.

extreme left; to its right, legend in Brāhmī in two horizontal lines having three letters each; (i) *putra ka* (ii) *ṇikas[ya]*. (*fig.* 2)

The legend on the obverse is quite clear on the coin; it is however not so clear in the photograph; but there is no doubt about its reading. The legend on the reverse is not so clear. There the first letter looks more like *sa* than *pu*, the lower stroke being battered; but than the second letter is clearly *tra* having the right lower stroke curved to left; so, it could not be simply *ta*; so I prefer to read the first letter as *pu* and the two letters together as *putra*. The alternate reading of the two letters may be *sata (s[u]ta)*. In both the cases, the word would mean the same thing, i.e., 'son'. The third letter, though not very clear, may be read as *ka*. In the second line, the first letter is clearly *ṇa* half in size of the other letters, with traces of a vertical stroke below the lower horizontal arm; and it may be taken as the stroke for medial *u*, but most likely it is meant for *i* and is erroneously placed with the lower arm instead of the upper one. It follows by a clear *ka* and then *sa*. The right hand vertical arm of *sa* has the traces of a curved stroke to the left at the lower end; this stroke suggests that there was a conjunct *ya*.

A legend divided on the two sides of a coin, is probably unknown anywhere in Indian numismatics; yet I venture to suggest that the legends on the obverse and reverse of this coin can be read meaningfully only when they are put together and read as *Huviṣkasya putra Kaṇikasya*. In this form, the legend may conveniently be compared to the legends on the coins of the Indo-Parthian rulers Aspavarma,[3] Zeionises,[4] Kharahoṣtes[5] and of the coins of the Western Kṣatrapas, where the names of the issuers are found with the names of their fathers. This legend, however, differs from them, in not having the word *putra* in genetive. To this it may be pointed out that in the hybrid Sanskrit, this form is not unusual. So far as I remember, some of the Mathura inscriptions of the Śaka-Kuṣāṇa period have this use. On coins of Spalahore, we have the nominative *Maharajabharata* (parallel to *putra*) along with the genetives *Dhramikasa*

Spalahorasa.[6] The exact parallel is seen on the coins of the Traikuṭakas of the later period, who copied the coinage of the Western Kṣatrapas. There we have the nominative *Mahārājendraputra......Dahrasena*[7] and.......*Dahrasenaputra..... Vyâghrasena.*[8] Thus the legend by itself poses no problem.

The only problem is, who was the issuer of this coin? The legend may have dual interpretation. If the two parts of the legend on the two sides are taken in continuation, beginning from the obverse and ending on the reverse, it would mean that Kaṇika was the issuer of coin and he was the son of Huviṣka. But if the two parts of the legend be taken as separate, it may then be interpreted as 'of Huviṣka' and 'son of Kaṇika'. In that case, the name on the obverse, i.e., Huviṣka would be that of the issuer and then according to the reverse legend, he would be the son of Kaṇika. But this latter interpretation seems unlikely as *putra kaṇikasya* in the sense of 'son of Kaṇika' is an unusual construction; proper construction in this sense would be *Kaṇikasya putra.* So, here the *putra* should go with *Huviṣkasya.* As such I believe that the issuer of this coin was Kaṇika, the son of Huviṣka.[9]

The coin has been discovered very close to Mathura, the capital of the Kuṣāṇas. Then the Kuṣāṇa structures laid immediately under the surface in the area of the find of the coin. From the point of palaeography, the coin cannot be later than the Kuṣāṇas. Above all, the names Huviṣka and Kaṇika[10] are the well-known names of the Imperial Kuṣāṇa rulers. All these facts leave no doubt that the coin relates to the Imperial Kuṣāṇa dynasty.

It is a needless to say that Kaṇika stands for Kaniṣka at many places in literature.[11] So, it may conveniently be suggested that the coin was issued by a Kaniṣka, who was the son of Huviṣka. Kaniṣka, the issuer of this coin would either be Kaniṣka I or Kaniṣka III as Kaniṣka II is already known as the son of Vajheṣka from Ārā Inscription.

B.N. Mukherji is of the opinion that the coin should be

attributed to Kaniṣka III, who was the successor of Vāsudeva I. His suggestion is based on two facts that (i) no imperial Kuṣāṇa coin has so far been known bearing a legend in Brāhmī. It is only on some coins of Vāsudeva I and his successors that have some stray letters in Brāhmī script.[12] So, this Brāhmī legend may be interpreted as an indication of an issue by a later Kuṣāṇa ruler in a period when Brāhmī has taken place of Kuṣāṇo-Bactrian script; (ii) A king Huviṣka is known to have ruled after Kaniṣka between the years 28 to 60. Besides these, some stylisation in the forms of the letters may also be considered as an indication of its being a late issue.[13]

But I see hardly any reason to attribute the coin to Kaniṣka III. There are certain other considerations that do not validly allow to place the coin in any late Kuṣāṇa period. The obverse device within a square incuse is a feature of early Indian numismatics which is unknown in any later period. It is known at the latest on the coins of the Pañcāla series, which ended with the advent of the Kuṣāṇas. Secondly, the human figure, though wears a foreign dress, is more akin to the figures on the early indigenous coins[14] than any effigy of the Kuṣāṇa rulers. Thirdly, the absence of the royal title reminds of the early local coinage. Fourthly, no Kuṣāṇa king had ever used patronymics on their coins, whereas it is seen on the coins of Mathura. Kṣatrapa Śodāsa (*Rājuvulaputasa Khatapasa Śodāsasa*).[15] These facts undoubtedly place the coins at the beginning of the Kuṣāṇa rule in the Mathura region. Besides these facts, it should also be borne in mind that the name Kaṇika is used in literature only for Kaniṣka I. I feel therefore, that this coin was issued by Kaniṣka I; perhaps he had experimented the issue of his coins in the indigenous style.

If it is so, the coin is historically very important and reveals a fact unknown so far, viz. the father of Kaniṣka I was Huviṣka. This Huviṣka might or might not have been ruler at any time; as there is no positive evidence that Kaniṣka I was the immediate successor of Vima Kadphises.[14]

References

1. B.M. Mukherjee has noticed this coin earlier in the *A.S.M.B.*, II, No. 8 (August 1973), pp. 5-6, based on my information and with my consent.
2. It may also be long hair hanging down to his shoulders, as B.N. Mukherjee thinks (*op. cit.*, p. 5).
3. *P.M.C.*, 1, p. 150.
4. *Ibid.*, p. 157.
5. *Ibid.*, p. 159.
6. *Ibid.*, p. 141, coin 372 etc.
7. *B.M.C.A.K.*, p. 198.
8. *Ibid.*, p. 202.
9. B.N. Mukherjee also holds the same opinion (*op. cit.*, p. 6).
10. B.N. Mukherjee, *The Kushana Genealogy*, p. 68; 104; 155; *The Kuṣāṇas and the Deccan*, p. 69.
11. For references, see supra p. fns 4-15.
12. *The Kushana Genealogy*, pp. 84f.
13. This is suggested by Härtel in one of his letters to the author.
14. Compare with the figure on coins, *B.M.C.,A.I.*, pl. XXXVII. 1-4.
15. *B.M.C.,A.I.*, p. 191,
16. See also Infra pp. 161ff.

6

Kuṣāṇa-Muruṇḍa Rule in Eastern India*

SOME Jain traditions refer to Muruṇḍa rule at Pāṭaliputra and there is some mention in Chinese and Tibetan works that Kaniṣka led a campaign into India, overthrew the kings of Sāketa and Pāṭaliputra and took away with him the Buddhist scholar Aśvaghoṣa. These references in literature have led some scholars to believe in the Kuṣāṇa rule in Bihar; they have tried to substantiate it by eliciting evidences from numismatics, epigraphy and plastic art.

Numismatics was employed to substantiate this idea, most likely for the first time, by K.P. Jayaswal. In his Presidential Address to the 26th Annual Conference of the Numismatic Society of India, he mentioned a find of a thousand Kuṣāṇa copper coins at Radhia in Motihari (Champaran) district (Bihar) and claimed that it proved the extension of the Kuṣāṇa rule up to Champaran; he also added that it lent support to the conclusion that he had earlier mentioned in his *History of Nepal*. This conclusion was that a century, which is a gap in Nepalese history, was probably covered by Kuṣāṇa rule whose coins were dug in Nepal. Since these coins were only a few, he then took their evidence as inconclusive; now the Radhia find established Kuṣāṇa rule in Champaran; and it also covered their rule in Nepal.[1] R.D. Banerji, on the basis of the coins in Orissa, came out, almost at the same time, with the suggestion that the Kuṣāṇas ruled in Orissa as far as the Ṛṣikulyā and Lāṅguliyā rivers.[2]

---

* Originally published in *Journal of the Numismatic Society of India*, XXXVIII (1976), pp. 25-53.

When A.S. Altekar published the hoard of Kuṣāṇa copper coins from Buxar, on the basis of that hoard and the finds of the Kuṣāṇa coins in the Pāṭaliputra excavations, he came out with the suggestion, that Vima Kadphises succeeded in conquering northern India right up to Patna. The Kuṣāṇa currency succeeded in completely ousting the indigenous copper currency in about 75 A.D.[3] He repeated the same views, but this time a little cautiously, when he published a gold amulet of the pattern of a Kuṣāṇa coin found at Sadargalli in Patna city. In this paper he referred to the same finds that he had mentioned in his earlier paper and said that on that evidence some scholars, including himself, hold that the Kuṣāṇa rule was *probably* well established in Bihar and Orissa at least for a few decades.[4]

Taking cue from Altekar, Adris Banerji, published two papers on the subject; one in the *Journal of the Numismatic Society of India*[5] and the other in the *Indian Historical Quarterly*.[6] In them he furnished a long list of the finds of the Kuṣāṇa coins in Eastern India and supplemented it with a list of epigraphic material and art relics of the Kuṣāṇa period known in this region and suggested that U.P., Bihar and possibly the Gangetic Delta in Bengal as well as Orissa were included for a time within the empire of Kaniṣka.

Lately, Sarjug Prasad Singh has published a long paper,[7] therein he has produced a long list of numismatic finds in Bengal, Bihar and Orissa, reiterated the Jain and Tibetan traditions, referred to some terracotta figurines and art-motifs from various sites in Bihar and said a few other things to stress that Bihar, Bengal and Orissa were included in the Kuṣāṇa-Muruṇḍa dominion. But he is not clear in his mind about his findings. Suggesting the inclusion of these eastern provinces in the Kuṣāṇa-Muruṇḍa dominion, he has used the word *possibility*, which simply meant that he was not sure about it. But most likely, he did not mean this; he believed firmly otherwise. He has asserted emphatically that Muruṇḍas were the viceroys of the eastern provinces of the Kuṣāṇa empire. This tends to suggest that Muruṇḍas were not the same as the Kuṣāṇas (as believed by many scholars); the Kuṣāṇas did not rule the east personally but through their viceroys, who were Muruṇḍas. Along with this, he has further suggested that the Muruṇḍa viceroys were empowered to issue their coins; these Muruṇḍa viceroys issued Purī-Kuṣāṇa coins; and Purī-Kuṣāṇa coins should actually be called Muruṇḍa coins. S.P. Singh has thus gone many steps ahead of other scholars in championing the Kuṣāṇa rule in the east.

Kuṣāṇa rule over Bihar and the regions to the east of it is not acceptable to many; I am one of them. In two papers[8] I have critically examined the numismatic material adduced by Altekar and Adris Banerji in support of their suggestions. In a third paper, I reviewed Altekar's views based on the Sadargalli amulet.[9] To me, there is no numismatic evidence that could suggest Kuṣāṇa expansion in the east beyond Vārāṇasī. I doubt even that much extent of the Kuṣāṇa empire on a number of considerations.

S.P. Singh has occasionally quoted Altekar but not Adris Banerji. I wonder, if he missed his papers or has deliberately overlooked them. Had he cared to see them, he would have perhaps added a few more finds to his list. He had perhaps no occasion to know my papers; otherwise, they would have helped him to correct some of the errors in his list and also given him some points to think over before putting into writing all that he has said. In any case, he has provided an occasion to review the matter afresh and to see if there is any reason to revise my views.

The list of the numismatic finds, produced by S.P. Singh, to prove the extension of the Kuṣāṇa empire into Bihar, Bengal and Orissa, is very much unbalanced in its contents. The list of the finds from Bihar is unnecessarily descriptive and contains such things as have no value for the present quest. It is an unnecessary waste of labour.[10] On the other hand, the finds from Bengal and Orissa are so briefly referred that they lack many valuable pieces of information.[11] Above all, it is a hotchpotch of several kinds of numismatic material uncritically accumulated. It includes: (a) coins — gold and copper; (b) looped or hooked gold coins meant for use as ornaments; and (c) gold coin-imitations or amulets, meant for ornaments or otherwise. Then the coins relate to three different sources: (a) stray finds; (b) finds in the form of hoards; and (c) discovered in course of archaeological excavations. It need hardly be said that the materials, belonging to these different categories do not have the same value or the same meaning for history. So, mere listing of these numismatic finds is not enough in a paper like the one presented by S.P. Singh. It is essential that the finds are properly classified and analysed; the analysis is put to proper interpretation; and their historical value is assessed; and then on the basis of this kind of assessment conclusions are arrived at. As such the list of the numismatic material placed by S.P. Singh in the form it is presented, is liable to mislead the readers.[12] It needs careful re-arrangement before its contents could be accepted for any historical conclusion.

Therefore the finds are re-described, classified into categories, according to their nature, and such informations are added as lacking with S.P. Singh. It includes also such finds that he has missed to note or were not known to him so that the material could be known in its entirety and the assessment could be fair.

GOLD AMULETS OR MEDALLIONS

1. **Bodh Gayā find:** A thin disc of gold showing the effigy of Huviṣka on both sides and looped at the top, was found by Cunningham in a deposit below the *Vajrāsana* at Bodh Gayā.[13]

2. **Kumrahāra find:** A fragmentary amulet showing a Kusāṇa king standing on one side and the goddess seated on the reverse was found in the excavations at Kumrahāra (Pāṭaliputra).[14] The motifs show that they were copied from some coin of the later Kuṣāṇa (post-Vāsudeva) ruler, which bear Ardokṣo seated on a high-backed throne.

3. **Sadargalli find:** A thin piece of gold, showing Huviṣka on the obverse and standing Ardokṣo on the reverse, with two holes at the top, was discovered in excavations at Sadargalli in Patna City.[15]

4. **Śiśupālgarh find:** In 1948, during archaeological excavations at Śiśupālgarh (Orissa), a gold piece was found, which bears a Kuṣāṇa coin-motif (i.e., King standing offering oblation) on one side and a Roman motif (i.e., Head of a king) on the other.[16] It bears a loop at the top. Altekar published this piece for the first time and took it to be a coin; On this piece he has tried to read Brāhmī legend *[Mahara]ja Rājadhasa Dhamadamadhara[sa]* (?) on the Kuṣāṇa motif side and some letters **HAIEAI. ZNAI** on the Roman motif side. He attributed it, as a coin, to *Mahārājā Rājādhirāja* Dharmadamadhara. Following him, everyone takes it to be a coin issued by an Orissan ruler. But actually the piece is not a coin. Both Kuṣāṇa and Roman coins were known in Orissa. Kuṣāṇa coin-motif had been imitated by the Guptas and the others; likewise the Roman-head motif was adopted by Sātavāhanas for their silver coins. Apparently, there is nothing unusual in the imitation of these motifs from two sources on this piece. But we have yet to find an instance where a mule of two different series of coins was used as coin. Had it been a coin issued by any ruler of Orissa, he would have adopted only one of the two coins as the prototype for his issues. It would have then been either a Kuṣāṇa or a Roman coin. There are a few other points which negativate its nature as a coin. A careful observation of the two sides of the piece would show that the legends from the original coins are meaninglessly copied. What Altekar has taken to be Brāhmī legend is nothing but the scribbling of the Kuṣāṇa legend in the same way as the Roman legend is scribbled on the Roman side. The title *Mahārāja rājatirāja,* no doubt, was used by the Kuṣāṇas in their inscriptions which were confined to Mathura and to its west. They never used this title on their coins. To trace out this legend on any piece found far away from Mathura, is merely an imagination.

The loop attached to the piece clearly shows that it was meant to be used as ornament. Mules of two different coin-motifs were often used on medallions, meant for decoration or ornament. An exact parallel to the present piece is in the British Museum collection. It was shown to me by G.K. Jenkins, when I had been there in 1972. It has a Roman head on one side and a Kuṣāṇa motif (standing Ardokṣo) on the other. When, how and where from it came to the Museum is not known; but there are reasons to believe that it originated in North-western Europe, in a Scandinavian country, most likely in Sweden in about the 5th century A.D.[17]

This does not mean that the present piece would also have been originated in Europe; but it does show that if a Swedish can fancy Roman and Kuṣāṇa motifs for his decoration; an Orissan had far better chances to be fascinated with the Kuṣāṇa and Roman motifs. The piece should be treated only as an amulet or decorative medallion, never a coin.

GOLD COINS AS ORNAMENTS

1. **Belwādāgā find:** A find of three Kuṣāṇa coins is reported by S.C. Roy from Belwādāgā in Ranchi district.[18] According to him, one of them was sold by the finder to some Zamindar; the other was given to some gold-smith and the third came to him. One of them (most likely the one that was obtained by Roy) related to Huviṣka and had a small gold pin or crown at the top. This suggests that the coin was used as an ornament. The details of other two coins are not known; but in view of this coin, it is not unlikely that they too might have had some similar attachments at the top and were used as ornaments.

2. **Sultanganj find:** A later Kuṣāṇa and a Gupta coin (Samudragupta: Standard type), both looped at the top, were found along with some ornaments in a pot at Sultanganj, Bhāgalpur district in 1959.[19]

3. **Lohārdāgā find:** Two Kuṣāṇa coins, both looped at the top with hollow tubes (meant for piercing string), were discovered as treasure trove along with a lump of gold at Lohārdāgā (District Ranchi) some time in 1965-96; they are now deposited in the Patna Museum. One of them is a double stater of Vima Kadphises and the other is a stater most probably of Vāsudeva. Both of them are very much worn.

GOLD COINS

Bihar

1. **Bhagalpur find:** Some gold coins of Vāsudeva were found in Bhāgalpur district in 1835.[20]

2. **Pāṭaliputra find:** Two gold coins, one of Vāsudeva with *Oeṣo* reverse and the other of some later Kuṣāṇa ruler (probably Kaniṣka III) with Ardokṣo seated on high backed throne, were found in excavations at Pāṭaliputra in 1912-13.[21]

3. **Mathia Puraria find:** 18 Kidāra-Kuṣāṇa coins were found in 1920 at the village Puraria (Rafiganj) district Gayā. Some of them had the letters *Pare* on the right and some others had only letter *sa*.[22]

4. **Monghyr find:** R.K. Chaudhury had seen three gold coins with a gold-smith at Monghyr, which he has described.[23] One of them was the coin of Samudragupta (Standard type) and the other two were Kuṣāṇa. One of the Kuṣāṇa coins belonged to Huviṣka and the other was a post-Vāsudeva coin, most probably of Kaniṣka III.

Bengal

5. **Mahāsthān find:** Two gold coins, one of Vāsudeva and the other unassigned were found at Mahāsthān. They were noticed by N.G. Majumdar.[24]

6. **Malda find:** A gold coin of Vāsudeva is reported by N.G. Majumdar as a find from Malda.[25]

7. **Murshidabad district find:** A coin of Vāsudeva in debased gold was found somewhere in Murshidabad district in 1890.[26]

8. **Bogra district find:** A gold Coin of Vāsudeva was found in 1909 in Bogra district.[27]

Madhya Pradesh

Harda find: Two gold coins (one quarter-stater of Huviṣka and the other stater of Kaniṣka III with *Oeṣo* reverse and the letters *ha, tha, aum*) were found at Harda in Hoshangabad district in the last quarter of the last century.[28]

COPPER COINS

North Bihar – North of the river Gaṅgā

1. **Belwa find:** In 1919, three Kuṣāṇa copper coins, including one of Kaniṣka, were found in archaeological diggings at Belwa (Subdivision Gopalganj), district Saran.[29]

2. **Chirand find:** In the archaeological excavations, that was conducted by Bihar State Archaeological department, a hoard of 88 Kuṣāṇa copper coins was found at Chirand in Saran district on the bank of the Gaṅgā.[30]

3. **Laghusā find:** A hoard of several hundred Kuṣāṇa copper coins, mixed with the Bull-Cock type coins of Ayodhyā, was found in an earthen pot at the village Laghusā (Gopalganj subdivision) district Saran. A few coins of both the types were presented to the Patna Museum some time between 1963 and 1972 by a resident of that village.[31]

4. **Lauria Nandangarh finds:** (a) In the archaeological excavations during 1935-36 a coin of Huviṣka (?)[32] and during 1936-37 two Kuṣāṇa coins (one of Kaniṣka and the other of Huviṣka)[33] were found at Lauria Nandangarh, district Champaran. (b) In 1939 a hoard consisting of 48 Kuṣāṇa (44 of Kaniṣka and 4 of Huviṣka) along with 14 Kuṣāṇa imitations of Punjab type was found there.[34] Most of the coins of this hoard are in the Patna Museum.

5. **Cherithan find:** In or about 1952 a small hoard of Kuṣāṇa copper coins was found at Cherithan in Champaran district and came in the possession of Ganesh Chaube of Bangri.[35]

6. **Radhia find:** In 1936, an earthen pot containing about a thousand Kuṣāṇa copper coins was found two feet below the ground by a villager while he was digging *kankar* in the village Radhia in Champaran district.[36] Seven coins from this find were acquired by the Patna Museum.[37]

7. **Vaiśālī finds:** In the archaeological excavations conducted

during 1911-12, only one copper coin of Vima Kadphises was found.[38] Again when in 1958-62 excavations were done there, 9 Kuṣāṇa coins (2 of Vima Kadaphises, 3 of Kaniṣka, 3 of Huviṣka, 1 later Kuṣāṇa) were found.[39] Some stray finds of Kuṣāṇa coins from this place are also known in the Vaiśālī Museum.[40]

8. **Utara find:** A hoard of 500 Kuṣāṇa copper coins was discovered at the village Utara (Janakpur), district Darbhanga, in the later part of the fifties, while digging a tank.[41]

Western Bihar — Border of U.P.

9. **Buxar find:** In 1949 a hoard containing 402 copper coins was found buried near the bank of the river Ganga at Buxar. It is published by Altekar.[42] It contained 23 coins of Vima Kadphises, 159 of Kaniṣka, 172 of Huviṣka, 23 undecipherable Kuṣāṇa, and 10 coins of Ayodhyā (Kosala) (Bull-Cock type).

South Bihar — South of Gaṅgā, Magadha

10. **Pāṭaliputra find:** In excavations at the ancient site of Pāṭaliputra in 1912-13[43] three Kuṣāṇa copper coins and in 1913-14[44] 52 Kuṣāṇa copper coins were discovered. None of these coins is described in detail; but Altekar has listed 45 coins of these finds, kept in the Patna Museum. They are: 3 of Vima Kadphises 13 of Kaniṣka and 30 of Huviṣka.[45] In the excavations conducted during 1951-55, 7 Kuṣāṇa coins were found at this site; 2 belonged to Kaniṣka, 4 to Huviṣka, and one unattributable.[46]

Chhota Nagpur region — Ancient Jharkhand

11. **Masubazar find:** 281 Purī-Kuṣāṇa coins were found at Masubazar, 32 miles south of Purulia. They are now in the Indian Museum, Calcutta.[47]

12. **Manbhum District find:** 93 Purī-Kuṣāṇa coins were found somewhere in Manbhum district.[48] Most probably this is the same find which P. Acharya has mentioned as the find from Birbhum,[49] a place in this very district.

13. **Kositanar find:** 130 Kuṣāṇa coins (110 of Kaniṣka, 19 worn and one unidentifiable) were found at Kositanar in Giridih Sub-division, district Hazaribagh in 1945.[50]

14. **Karra find:** A copper coin of Kaniṣka is noticed as the find from Karra in Ranchi district.[51]

15. **Kusumbagan find:** In May 1928, 12 Purī-Kuṣāṇa coins were found at Kusumbagan, near Rakha Hill mines in Singhbhum district. The coins are in the Patna Museum.[52]

16. **Maholia find:** 26 Purī-Kuṣāṇa coins were found in 1931 at Maholia (Swaspur) in Singhbhum district.[53]

17. **Pindrabera find:** A big hoard of Purī-Kuṣāṇa coins was found by the side of a river at the village Pindrabera (Saraikela-Kharsawan), district Singhbhum, in 1952. Since most of the coins were rusted and decomposed only 20 coins were acquired by Patna Museum.[54]

18. **Rakha Hills find:** 363 Purī-Kuṣāṇa coins were found as a hoard on the northern slope of the Rakha Hills in Singhbhum district in 1917. Three of the coins were inscribed as *Leṅka* or *Taṅka*.[55]

Orissa

19. **Balasore find:** 910 Purī-Kuṣāṇa coins were discovered in Balasore district. They are now in the Indian Museum, Calcutta.[56] One of the coins had the legend as found on a few coins of find No. 18 mentioned above.

20. **Śiśupālgarh find:** 2 Kuṣāṇa (1 of Kaniṣka and 1 of Huviṣka) and 4 Purī-Kuṣāṇa coins were found in the excavations at Śiśupālgarh in Bhubaneshwar in 1948.[57]

21. **Cuttack District find:** 26 Purī-Kuṣāṇa coins were found somewhere in Cuttack district in 1931-32.[58]

22. **Kayema find:** 13 Kuṣāṇa (Kaniṣka and Huviṣka) coins were found near the foot of Kayema Hills in the Jaypur Sub-division in Cuttack district.[59]

23. **Purusottampur find:** A hoard of Kuṣāṇa and Purī-Kuṣāṇa coins was found in the neighbourhood of Purusottampur in Ganjam district in 1858. These coins were studied by W. Elliot.[60]

24. **Jaugada and Gulka finds:** J.D. Beglar had found some Indo-Scythian (Kuṣāṇa) coins at Jaugada and Gulka near Purusottampur in Ganjam district.[61]

25. **Sitabhanji finds:** 135 Kuṣāṇa and Purī-Kuṣāṇa coins were found in a hoard at Sitabhanji in Keonjhar district.[62] Thereafter, L.N. Bhanjadeva of Keonjhar discovered from this area some Kuṣāṇa and Purī-Kuṣāṇa copper coins.[63] T. Ramachandran had also found 5 Purī-Kuṣāṇa coins here.[64]

26. **Bhanjakiā finds:** Three hoards of Kuṣāṇa and Purī-Kuṣāṇa coins are known to have been found at Bhanjakiā (Panchipidha) in district Mayurbhanj. One was found in 1923; but the exact number of the coins is not known.[65] The second one was found in 1927 and contained 22 Purī-Kuṣāṇa coins.[66] This find perhaps included two inscribed coins.[67] Later in 1953, 1261 Purī-Kuṣāṇa coins along with a coin of Kaniṣka were found.[68]

27. **Nuagaon find:** In May 1939, 105 Purī-Kuṣāṇa coins were found in a brass pot at Nuagaon, near Joshipur-Bhanjakiā in Mayurbhanj district.[69]

28. **Virāṭgarh find:** Kuṣāṇa and Purī-Kuṣāṇa coins were found in excavations at Virāṭgarh in Khiching in Mayurbhanj district.[70]

29. **Mayurbhanj District find:** R.D. Banerji has mentioned a find of a hoard of 282 copper coins (112 Kuṣāṇa and 170 Purī-Kuṣāṇa) from the Mayurbhanj district.[71]

30. **Māṇika Pātaṇā find:** 84 Kuṣāṇa and Purī-Kuṣāṇa coins were found in a hoard at Gauribari Salt Factory, near Māṇika-Pātaṇā in Puri district in 1893.[72]

31. **Nayagarh State find:** Some Purī-Kuṣāṇa coins were found in erstwhile Nayagarh State in the last century.[73]

Andhra Pradesh

32. **Bhilingi find:** 100 Purī-Kuṣāṇa copper coins were found at Bhilingi in Srikakulam district, of which five were published.[74]

Kosala -- East Madhya Pradesh and North-East Maharashtra

33. **Kenda Zamindari find:** 25 Kuṣāṇa copper coins were found in 1922 at the old Kenda Zamindari in Bilaspur district. Almost all the coins were worn out; only four belonging to Kaniṣka and Huviṣka were acquired by the Nagpur Museum.[75]

34. **Jhajhapuri find:** Fifteen Kuṣāṇa copper coins were found by a villager (?) in 1954 in the village Jhajhapuri (Mungeli), district Bilaspur.[76] Two coins of this find are in the Nagpur Museum.

35. **Pendarwa find:** Some Kuṣāṇa copper coins along with Yaudheya (?) coins were found in 1952 at the village Pendarwa (Chandrapur) in Bilaspur district.[77] They were with the late Pandey Lochan Prasad Sharma.

36. **Tewar (Tripurī) find:** A copper coin of Vāsudeva was found at Tripurī near Jabalpur.[78]

37. **Shahdol find:** A hoard of 757 Kuṣāṇa copper coins was discovered in 1965 in Shahdol district. It contained 44 coins of Vima Kadphises, 324 of Kaniṣka and 362 of Huviṣka; the remaining 27 were unidentifiable. All the coins were very much worn.[79]

38. **Katangi find:** A hoard of 8 Kuṣāṇa copper coins was found in January 1973 at Village Katangi, Taluka Gondia, district Bilaspur.[80]

Bengal

39. **Tāmluk find:** A copper coin of Kaniṣka was found in 1882 at Tāmluk in Midnapur district.[81]

S. Chattopadhyaya informs that some copper coins of Kuṣāṇa type, collected from the southern districts of Bengal, were in the Directorate of Archaeology, Bengal.[82] Though the provenance is not properly disclosed, it may be guessed that the coins might have come from some place bordering either Chhota Nagpur region of Bihar or of Orissa.

This long list of finds of Kuṣāṇa numismatic material would

apparently suggest that the Kuṣāṇa rule extended not only over Bihar, Bengal and Orissa, but also over Andhra Pradesh, Madhya Pradesh and North-Eastern Maharashtra. But here it is to be realised that the finds grouped under categories A and B, being in the nature of ornaments, are no direct evidence for any conclusion related to political history. Any type of coin, without any consideration of time and place, may fascinate people to adopt it as ornament or copy it for the same purpose. It is not necessary that prototype for an amulet or the medallion should be the coin of the period when it was being prepared or of the ruler who was ruling then or in whose domain it was being prepared. It need hardly be said that Romans were never rulers in India yet Roman coins found favour with the people in this country and they imitated those coins in metal and clay and made ornaments with loops, similar to those described above under Category A.

At Nāgārjunīkoṇḍā, in *Stūpa* No. 6, among the relics were found two tiny coin-like gold medallions; each one had two holes at the top like the Sadargalli medallion. One had the effigy of a woman and the other of a young man, both showed marked Roman influence.[83] Imitations of Roman coins in clay are known from many sites in India, viz, Śiśupālgarh (Orissa),[84] Rājghāṭ (Vārāṇasī),[85] Kauśāmbi (Allahabad),[86] Ujjain (Madhya Pradesh),[87] Karād (district Satara),[88] Brahmapuri (Kolhapur),[89] Bhokardan,[90] Koṇḍapur (Andhra Pradesh),[91] Candravalli (Mysore).[92] At some of these places Roman coins were never current.

Similarly, the Venetian ducats or sequins, that came to India by way of trade in the fourteenth century A.D. were also imitated by people for the same purpose. Indian made dies for making these imitations were found in the Kaira district of Gujarat.[93] An interesting imitation is in the Madras Museum.[94] The Prince of Wales Museum, Bombay, possesses about a dozen brass imitations of the Venetian ducats with loops at the top.[95] As late as 1882, imitations of the sequins were common in Maharashtra for ornamental purposes; large number of women of the lower and middle classes wore them round their necks.[96] They called it *putalī*.

Again, silver coins of Shah Alam II were imitated on a large scale and were produced by the Vārāṇasī silversmiths as late as fifties; and they were used as necklace by the village women of the surrounding districts. They are called *Hamel.* Even now, the gold *Gajapati* pagoda (Elephant on the obverse and floral scroll on the reverse) is favourite with the South Indian high class women for necklace.

The Kuṣāṇa amulets and medallions, listed above under the finds of category A, may be the parallel instances. They might or might not have been prepared in the period when the Kuṣāṇas were ruling in North India. Similarly, they may or may not have been prepared at the places where they have been found or in their vicinity; they might have come from outside through trade.

Very much the same may be said about the use of the original coins as ornaments, the finds of which are mentioned under category B. The *Muhars* of Akbar may still be seen adoring the necks of village people. It would not be out of place to mention that the Mahārāja of Bharatpur was so much fascinated with the Gupta gold coins, when the find of the Bayana hoard was brought before him, that he has asked the officer-in-charge of his treasury, to get their buttons made for him and his retinues; and he got a few buttons made for himself even after knowing their antique value. The Sultanganj find of the looped Gupta and Kuṣāṇa coins (find 2, Category B) together is by itself an evidence that the Kuṣāṇa coins were used as ornaments, even at the time when Gupta coins had become current.

Keeping these facts in view, the finds of the categories A and B cannot be cited as any positive evidence for the Kuṣāṇa rule in Bihar or its vicinity. They may by cited as circumstantial evidence, only if there are some other evidences to suggest such a possibility. Even then, let us examine these materials. Of the four finds of Category A and three finds of Category B, only two of the first and one of the second may be taken as having some relevance to the problem before us. The others can have no bearing on it as they relate to the coins which were issued in a period, when nobody, not even the champions of the Kuṣāṇa rule in

Bihar, think their existence, not only in Bihar but even in the major part of their kingdom. The finds (2 and 4 of Category A; 2 and 3 of Category B, relate to Vāsudeva or his successors. Vāsudeva's rule did not extend beyond Mathura. Altekar himself denies Vāsudeva's rule in Bihar. He thinks that Vāsudeva's coins were brought to Pāṭaliputra by traders and pilgrims in the third century A.D.[97] If the later Kuṣāṇa coins were coming to Bihar by way of trade, there is no reason why the coins of the earlier or Imperial Kuṣāṇas would not have come there in the same way. The Huviṣka medallions might be the results of the same kind of importation. But on the basis of the Sadargalli Huviṣka amulet Altekar had ventured to suggest that Kuṣāṇa currency was so common in Bihar that the ladies had taken fancy for some of its types and ordered goldsmiths to prepare pendants or talismans in imitation of them.[98] If it was so, then we should certainly have the Kuṣāṇa gold coins in Bihar in abundance; and this should be visible in the finds of Category C, i.e., the actual coins.

But the finds of Category C, known to us, are not more than four such coins from Bihar and the same number is known from Bengal. Here, again we find that most of the coins relate to Vāsudeva or his successors. All the Bengal finds relate to Vāsudeva.[99] They by themselves are no evidence for the rule of Kaniṣka and Huviṣka in Bengal. The same way be said for the finds from Bihar. The Bhagalpur and Pāṭaliputra finds relate to Vāsudeva and Mathia-Puraria find belongs to the Kidāra Kuṣāṇas, who were almost contemporary with the Gupta rulers in the Punjab. Coins of all these finds might have travelled into Bihar, earliest by the third century A.D. Now remains the Monghyr find. The nature of this find is so dubious that it is difficult to admit it for any evidence. We do not know if the coins, seen by Chaudhury with the Monghyr goldsmith, were found within the precincts of Bihar. But even if we admit that the coins were found in Bihar, there is nothing to suggest that they formed a hoard. If they belonged to one and the same source, then the value of this find is lost for the reason that it could not have been buried before the time of Samudragupta, whose coin is there. If the two Kuṣāṇa coins were found separate from the Gupta coin, even then position remains the same. It is only if we are sure that Huviṣka's coins was found alone that it may have some value. But then, does this sole coin of Huviṣka testifies Altekar's contention?

The rule of any king or dynasty at any place is generally admitted by numismatists and historians only when coins are found in substantial quantity and spread over a wide area within the territory, presumed to be under the domain. In the case of the Kuṣāṇa, in Uttar Pradesh, which undoubtedly formed part of the Kuṣāṇa dominion under Kaniṣka and Huviṣka, Kuṣāṇa coins of both the rulers in gold and copper are discovered off and on from every corner of the state and in substantial numbers. Had any part of Bihar been under the Kuṣāṇas, we should have had the extension of their coins in this region and then there would have been plenty of their coins and not only a single coin at Monghyr or a few ornaments, prepared out of the coins or their imitations, found elsewhere. The absence of the gold coins is most significant in itself; it should be enough to show that the Kuṣāṇas never penetrated in the east beyond the Gaṅgā.

But not much attention has been given to the paucity of the gold coins; what has been said on the problem, is mostly based on the copper coins. So let us see what the finds of the copper coins, listed under Category D, say on this point.

The list undoubtedly apparently shows that Kuṣāṇa coins were scattered over Bihar, Orissa, western Bengal, northern Andhra Pradesh and the eastern part of Madhya Pradesh, i.e., Kosala and Maharashtra; and there they were found in appreciable numbers. On their basis, Altekar,[100] Adris Banerji[101] and S.P. Singh[102] suggest Kusāṇa rule in Bihar. R.D. Banerji,[103] Dilip Kumar Ganguli[104] and S.C. Behera[105] speculate their rule in Orissa and B.C. Jain hints of the Kuṣāṇa dominion in Madhya Pradesh.[106] General belief amongst Indian numismatists had been that copper coins do not travel long, while gold and silver coins may be taken, by way of trade, to distant lands without implying any political occupation; the presence of copper coins in any place can only mean a political occupation. This fallacious belief[107] is at work behind these thinkings.

Before these views are analysed, it is necessary to point out that in ancient days Bihar was not the same as understood today in its political and geographical connotations. There were several states (*Janpadas*) within this geographical boundary before the rise of the Nanda-Maurya empire; and most likely, the same was the case after the decline of the Mauryas. Magadha was one of them and the foremost. It corresponded in the time of the Buddha to the modern district of Patna with the addition of the northern half of the Gaya district. The boundaries were probably the Gaṅgā to the north, the Son to the west, a dense forest reaching the plateau of Chhota Nagpur to the south and Aṅga to the east. The river Campā was the boundary between Magadha and Aṅga.[108] But according to Cunningham,[109] Magadha occupied a wider territory, bounded by the Gaṅgā on the north, by the district of Banaras (Vārāṇasī) on the west, Hiraṇya-parvāta or Monghyr in the east and by Karṇa-suvarṇa or Singhbhum on the south. The Tibetan traditions that refer to Kaniṣka's expedition of Pāṭaliputra, and the Jain traditions that mention Muruṇḍa rule in Pāṭaliputra, would have meant by Pāṭaliputra the state of Magadha, which was so bounded. As such to substantiate these traditions of Kuṣāṇa rule in Magadha, we should have a large number of coins particularly in this area, as we do have in the Uttar Pradesh. But to our utter dismay, we have only a few copper coins that were found in the excavations at Pāṭalipura.

The coins found in the excavations in 1912-13 are known to us today out of their context. It is only about the coins found during the excavations in 1951-55 that we know something of their context. They were found in the layers that the excavators date between 100 and 300 A.D. But we have no clear indications in the *Report* to know if these coins were found in the layers near to the lower limit of the date or the upper limit. Whatever might be the fact, even if the coins were found in the layers which may be definitely attributed to the early period, contemporaneous to the Kuṣāṇa rule in Uttar Pradesh, these few coins, found at only one place, could not be accepted as the evidence of the extension of the Kuṣāṇa rule in Magadha. They would certainly have had some value had we found a few, if not many coins, scattered all over the long stretch of the land between Vārāṇasī and Pāṭaliputra. A complete vacuum in this region tends to suggest only that the coins might have come to Pāṭaliputra, an important centre, by any means other than by the reason of any political dominance.

Altekar had laid great stress on the Buxar find, which was found on the bank of the Gaṅgā, just on the border of Uttar Pradesh and Bihar (Magadha in this case). But this hoard also does not disclose any indication of the Kuṣāṇa rule over the Magadha side of the Gaṅgā. The currency of the coins of a state in the lands of another state, touching the border is a very common phenomenon. The coins of the erstwhile princely state of Gwalior were in common currency outside the state as far as Agra on one side and up to Itarsi on the other. Likewise, even to this day, the coins of Nepal are freely accepted by the people residing in the neighbouring districts in India, situated in Uttar Pradesh and Bihar. This is simply for the reason of convenience of the people residing on either side of the borders. This would in no way mean the expansion of the Sindhias up to Agra or Itarsi or that of Nepal into India. Similar could well be the reason for the find of Kuṣāṇa coins at Buxar on the Gaṅgā. No political significance can be attached to it in absence of any other corroborative evidence.

Besides the complete isolation of the Buxar find from the finds of Pāṭaliputra, another noticeable feature of the Buxar hoard is that it was not exclusively Kuṣāṇa. It also contained the coins of the 'Bull-Cock type' of the Mitra rulers of Ayodhyā (Kosala). At Ayodhyā (Kosala), there was a continuous chain of indigenous rulers from the time of the Śuṅgas till at least the second century A.D. if not later. As such the Kuṣāṇas and the Mitra rulers were contemporary.[110] It is not expected that the Kuṣāṇa coins would be current with the local coins in the territories of Ayodhyā (Kosala) kingdom in the same period. If the coins of the two series are found in a hoard it would only mean (if the hoard is found in the territory of Ayodhyā) that the Kuṣāṇa coins overlapped the Ayodhyā coins. And the hoards found in the

Ayodhyā territory containing the coins of both the series, show that in them Ayodhyā coins are few and the Kuṣāṇa coins are in pre-dominance.[111] This shows that the Kuṣāṇa coins ousted the Ayodhyā coins towards the end of the second or the beginning of the third century A.D. This would in turn mean that the Kuṣāṇa coins entered Ayodhyā territory only after the fall of the Kuṣāṇa empire; and as such, the Buxar find has no bearing on the Kuṣāṇa occupation of Magadha, being dated in the post-Kuṣāṇa period.

If the hoards of the Kuṣāṇa coins, found in the territories of Ayodhyā kingdom, be taken as an indication of the political expansion of the Kuṣāṇa empire in the latter's territories, then the belief in the date of the accession of Kaniṣka in 78 A.D. will have to be dropped and the event will have to be placed some time in the second century A.D.[112] But even in that case, the isolated nature of the Buxar hoard would not indicate any expansion of the Kuṣāṇas in Magadha.

We have no numismatic evidence to suggest Kuṣāṇa rule in Magadha. If Kaniṣka had any successful expedition against Pāṭaliputra, as Chinese and Tibetan traditions make us believe, it left no scar whatsoever. They do not bear testimony to the inclusion of Eastern India in the Kuṣāṇa empire. Similarly, if the Muruṇḍas, mentioned in the Jain traditions, really ruled over Magadha, whosoever else they might have been, they could not be the Kuṣāṇas.

With these facts, if finds of the Kuṣāṇa copper coins, listed above under Category D, are taken to mean political expansion of the Kuṣāṇas in the east, they would only suggest that this expansion was two-pronged. One was in the continuation of the Kuṣāṇa territories in Uttar Pradesh, in the direction of north-east to the north of the river Gaṅgā in the districts of Saran, Champaran, Muzaffarpur and Darbhanga in Bihar (For convenience of reference, this area may be called *North Zone*). The other expansion was towards the south, south of Magadha. It comprised the Jharkhand part of Bihar, Orissa, western Bengal, north-eastern part of Andhra Pradesh, south-eastern part of

Madhya Pradesh (i.e., Kosala) (this area would be called hereafter in this paper as *South Zone*). There was thus a big gap, which formed an independent kingdom of Magadha, ruled by someone else, between these two zones of the Kuṣāṇa expansions in the east. The coin-finds further reveal that the southern expansion of the Kuṣāṇa kingdom was in the nature of an independent pocket, cut off from the main land of the empire, very much in the same way as in recent time we had for some time two Pakistans — east and west.

However, it is unthinkable of any expansion of northern India towards the east without Magadha and also to speak of an East Pakistan-like pocket, separated from the main kingdom, in any period of ancient Indian history. One must bear in mind that had the Kuṣāṇas occupied the lands on either side of Magadha, there would have been no reason for them to leave Magadha untouched. There was no power which could have prevented them from its occupation. The Kuṣāṇas would have never left Magadha out of their control.

The absence of the Kuṣāṇa coins from Magadha is a positive evidence to show the non-existence of the Kuṣāṇa hold over Magadha; so the presence of their coins on either side of Magadha cannot be accepted as evidence for the political domination of the Kuṣāṇas over any of the two territories (North and South zones) unless there is something else to support it. Mere theorising that the presence of copper coins means political occupation is not enough.[113] There could be many reasons and occasions, when they could be carried, like gold and silver coins, to distant lands. They all will have to be assessed before arriving at any conclusion of political significance.

In most of the finds of the South Zone, Kuṣāṇa coins have been found along with the Purī-Kuṣāṇa coins, which have been variously designated as Oriyā-Kuṣāṇa or Imitation Kuṣāṇa. It is, therefore, it was being suggested that the two series of coins were current in one and the same period. It has also been surmised that during the last phase of the Kuṣāṇa rule in India, when they were fighting with the forces of the rising Yaudheyas and other tribes in the second or third century A.D. in the Punjab-Rajasthan region, the supply of the Kuṣāṇa currency in some parts of eastern India became short and inadequate; then the viceroys of the eastern provinces of the Kuṣāṇa empire were empowered to issue coins in order to meet the shortage of the currency in the region. It is suggested that this South Zone was ruled by the Kuṣāṇas through their viceroys and these viceroys issued the Puri-Kuṣāṇa coins.[114] We have the instance of the Sassanians, who ruled their Indian territories through their governors; and these governors had issued their coins. So, this suggestion could have had some possibility, had there been some evidence to support any such assumption. Had Purī-Kuṣāṇa coins been issued by the Kuṣāṇa viceroys or governors, they should have been found distributed throughout the entire South Zone covered by the finds. The finds available to us show that Purī-Kuṣāṇa coins were confined only to Singhbhum district of Bihar, Orissa and a single find in Andhra Pradesh. They are conspicuously absent from all the finds in the Hazaribagh district of Bihar and all the finds of Bengal and Madhya Pradesh.

Again, had these coins been issued by the Kuṣāṇa governors, they should have been exactly of the type of the Kuṣāṇa coins and not merely their imitations, having just semblance of the motifs. The Sassanian governors issued coins in their provinces, and they were similar to the coins issued by the Sassanian emperors themselves, and not their imitations in any way. Then, this was the region, where copper mines are known and the metal is available in plenty. There was no need of any austerity; the coins would have been issued not only with the Kuṣāṇa motifs, but also of the same shape, size, and weight. These facts, speak themselves, that they were not issued by any Kuṣāṇa governor under any Kuṣāṇa imperial authority.

The Balasore, Rakha Hills and one of the Bhanjakiā finds (Nos. 19, 18 and 26 of Category D of the above list) had Purī-Kuṣāṇa coins, which were inscribed. The legend on the coins of Balasore and Bhanjakiā finds is nowhere described. The legend on Rakha Hills coins has been read as *leṅka* or *taṅka*; but this reading is uncertain. It is difficult to say if what has been read on the coins meant a denomination or the name of a place or person. However, for our purpose its palaeography is important. On its basis R.D. Banerji dates these coins some time earlier than the seventh century A.D.[115] But J. Allan does not think that the coins are so late. To him, the epigraphy can be paralleled in Samudragupta's Allahabad inscription. So, he dates the coins to the end of the third or early fourth century A.D.[116] T.N. Ramachandran places these coins in the fourth century A.D., as he found some coins near or in a rock-shelter, which bears a tempera painting, datable to this period.[117] In the excavations at Śiśupālgarh, the Purī-Kusāṇa coins were found in the layers which, according to the *Report,* are datable to 300-350 A.D.[118] Thus, Purī-Kuṣāṇa coins may reasonably and with certainty be placed at the earliest in the fourth century A.D.[119] And by this time, the Kuṣāṇa rule had dwindled into a small kingdom in the Punjab. So any Kuṣāṇa viceroy, ruling in this period in far east is mere imagination.

It is thus, clear that the Purī-Kuṣāṇa coins were issued by some local ruler or rulers who had hold over a small territory, confined only to Orissa and the adjoining fringes in Bihar and Andhra Pradesh. They borrowed the idea from the motifs of the Kuṣāṇa coins, then current there; but at the same time they had their own innovations in the matters of technique, fabric and weight. This makes it evident that the Kuṣāṇa coins were current there during this period or just before it in the third century A.D. Had the Kuṣāṇa coins been current there from the very beginning of the Kuṣāṇa rule in India or from the time of Kaniṣka and had a continued flow up to the third or fourth century A.D., there should have been in these finds, not only the coins of Kaniṣka and Huviṣka but also the coins of Vāsudeva, which are here conspicuously absent. This shows that the coins came to Orissa only when the rule of Vāsudeva had ceased to exist in Uttar Pradesh; and they came there only through trade and travel.

It need hardly be said that at this time Orissa and the

adjoining areas were serving as the gateway of India for the seafarers, who were going regularly to the far-east islands and whose accounts are narrated in stories and other literature. The route of Orissa from the Gaṅgā valley was not through Pāṭaliputra but from Vārāṇasī through Mirzapur; it went direct to Orissa crossing the Jharkhand region. I am not aware if this route is mentioned anywhere in literature; but in my studies, I came to realise this from several other sources. Working on the pre-historic copper hoard objects, I found that these objects are scattered almost all over the districts of Jharkhand and are extended up to Palamau district and then they are seen only in Vārāṇasī district in the Gaṅgā valley; and thence they had moved west to the Yamunā-Gaṅgā plains. They are unknown anywhere in Magadha and to its north.[120] Similarly, the finds of the silver punch-marked coins in southern Bihar show that these are distinctly cut off from their distribution in Magadha and the Gangetic plains and are seen in the Jharkhand region linked up with Vārāṇasī.[121] Lately, the contents of a hoard of Mughal coins, discovered in Palamau district, revealed that the area was more intimately connected with Vārāṇasī than with Patna and Dacca, the principal towns of the Mughal administration. The hoard contained large number of coins of Banaras mint and the mints to its west; and had only a few coins or perhaps none of Patna and Dacca mints.[122]

We do not get any trace of the Kuṣāṇa coins to the east of Vārāṇasī till we reach Orissa or its fringe in Bihar. One may pertinently question, if this was the ancient route to Orissa from Vārāṇasī, traces of it should also have been noticeable in the Kuṣāṇa finds. But traces are rarely available to indicate the trade-route. Coins are mostly found suddenly jumped from one area into another. For instance, Roman coins in South India are found without any trace on the whole route;[123] similarly the Kuṣāṇa coins found in Abyssinia[124] have left no trace anywhere in the way. Perhaps, these would not be appropriate instances to parallel with the present case. So, it may be pointed out that the Bent-bar coins of Gandhāra are known at Kauśāmbī,[125] without any trace all along the long route; similarly, the Local silver punch-marked coins of Śūrasena (Mathura) *janapada* are konwn in the distant Śrī Laṅkā (Ceylon).[126] The Indo-Greek coins are known far away from their context in the Hamirpur district in Uttar Pradesh.[127] In all these instances and in many other such instances, the finds of the coins are the results of commercial communications. They show that the coins of a territory are found in another territory only when and if the latter is an important trading centre, which in this case, Orissa was.

The North zone, i.e., the districts of Saran, Champaran, Muzaffarpur and Darbhanga in Bihar, where Kuṣāṇa coins have been found, are so congruous with the main lands of the Kuṣāṇa empire that their finds could well be taken as the result of political expansion. But that it was not so, apparent from at least three of the finds. The Laghusā find (Find No. 3) was very much similar to the Buxar find (Find No. 9) in its contents, i.e., it had the Kuṣāṇa coins along with the coins of the Mitra rulers of Ayodhyā; and the find-place also is likewise almost on the border of Uttar Pradesh. All the observations made in respect of the Buxar find will equally apply to it. It shows that the hoard had entered the Bihar region after the fall of the Kuṣāṇa empire.

The second is the Lauria Nandangarh find of the year 1937 (Find No. 4b), which included imitations of the Kuṣāṇa coins of the Punjab type along with the coins of the Imperial Kuṣāṇas. Here the presence of the Punjab imitations by itself shows that the coins entered the area long after the fall of the Kuṣāṇas, most likely in the fourth century A.D.

The last but the most important are the coin-finds from Vaiśālī, discovered in the excavations of 1958-62 (Find No. 7). The excavators have admitted in their *Report* that the Kuṣāṇa coins were found there in the layers of the late period. Reading in between the lines of the *Report* would convince anyone that the coins do not belong to the period when the Kuṣāṇa power was at its height.

The most important evidence that their spade has brought out has been missed by the excavators. It is the coin of Vima Kadphises, found in the excavations, counterstruck on both sides with a sign which appears like a bold **S**. (*fig. 1*) This bold **S** sign was the *tamghā* of the rulers of the Afrigian dynasty of Khwarizm (in Central Asia), which had succeeded the Kuṣāṇas there in or about the fourth century A.D. There these rulers had counterstruck the Kuṣāṇa coins with this **S** sign in plenty.[128] The find of a Kuṣāṇa coin with the counterstriking symbol of the Afrigian rulers of Khwarizm at Vaiśālī is an unimpeachable evidence not only to show that the Kuṣāṇa coins at Vaiśālī were current in the fourth century A.D., but also that the *copper coins did travel far and wide*. In this case the Vima Kadphises' coin, counterstuck with the *tamghā* of Afrigian rulers of Central Asia, had travelled all the way from Khwarizm to Vaiśālī, far east in India.

In the light of these observations it may well be visualised that the coins found in the hoards in the North as well as in the South Zone might also have come there in the same way from the Kuṣāṇa-occupied territories in post-Kuṣāṇa period. There is no numismatic evidence which could even slightly suggest any Kuṣāṇa expansion in the east in Bihar, Bengal and Orissa or anywhere else.[129]

The reason for the spread of the Kuṣāṇa copper coins after the fall of their empire in the Gupta period, is so apparent that it needs no dilation. The Guptas issued gold coins in profusion; but they were unable to meet the needs of the common people.[130] Their silver coins were few and were confined to Western and Central India and there, they too came into existence only towards the end of the fourth century A.D. in the time of Candragupta II. The Kuṣāṇas themselves had not issued silver coins. Copper coins of the Guptas were scarce. So, the people, who needed small currencies for meeting their needs, in the Gupta period, had no other course than to use the Kuṣāṇa copper coins, which were profuse and readily available. It is not unlikely that the Kuṣāṇa copper coins came to these eastern territories through trade not as any currency but as a commodity of need. The traders might have been selling or exchanging these copper coins at some premium and thus making a good profit for all the troubles they took to bring them from the west.

References

1. *Annual Report of the Numismatic Society of India*, 1936, p. 11; *Sixty years of the Numismatic Society of India*, p. 148.
2. *History of Orissa*, I, p. 115ff.
3. *J.N.S.I.*, XII, pp. 121-23; *Kumrahar Excavations*, 1951-55, p. 10.
4. *Ibid.*, XX, pp. 1-3.
5. *Ibid* XIII, pp. 107-09.
6. *I.H.Q.*, XXVI, pp. 294-303.
7. *J.N.S.I.*, XXXV, p. 127-41.
8. *Ibid.*, XV, p. 185; *IHQ*, XXIX, pp. 205-21; supra pp. 21-50.
9. *Ibid.*, XXI, p. 188-90; supra, p 83.
10. This list is in no way the result of any labour or research of the author. It is simply a copy of the relevant portions of the List of Coin-finds of Bihar and Orissa, prepared by H.K. Prasad, a colleague of mine at the Patna Museum, on the basis of the Treasure Trove records deposited in the Museum and the Coin-registers at my instance. It was published in *I.N.C.*, VIII, pp. 45-101. In absence of the proper acknowledgement to the source, his act is plagiary, highly deplorable.
11. Though the original sources are quoted by the author in the foot-notes, it seems that he had no access to them. He has, most probably, relied on the secondary sources where the finds are briefly or inadequately noticed.
12. It would be interesting to quote Tarn, who has given some thought to the use of numismatic material as evidence for history. He says, "Much use has been made by some writers of the find-spots of coins in determining where this or that king reigned, but it is not a satisfactory form of evidence .... Coins travel in trade and almost any other kind of evidence is preferable .... The following rules seem sound. If a king has an abundant coinage which is found in many places over great distances .... that is evidence of widely extended rule; but not evidence that he ruled in all the places where his coins are found. If the coins of a king with a very large coinage are never found in a particular district, that creates a presumption, in the absence of other evidence, that he did not rule there; but if coinage is small, no presumption is created; and in both cases, large and small coinage, the absence of coinage in a district cannot be set up against other evidence .... If only a few isolated coins of a king be known, the find-spot affords no real evidence for the locality of his rule." *The Greeks in Bactria and India*, p. 440; *see* also A.K. Narain, Numismatic Evidence and Historical Writing, *J.N.S.I.*, XVIII, II, pp. 157-62, on this and other related issues.
13. Cunningham, *Mahābodhi*, Pl. XXII, fig. 17.

14. *Kumrahar Excavations,* 1951-55, p. 131.
15. *J.N.S.I.,* XX, pp. 1-3; *Pāṭaliputra Excavations 1955-56,* pp. 52-53; supra, p. 51ff.
16. *Ibid.,* XII, pp. 1-4; *Ancient India,* No. 5, p. 97; S.P. Singh has identified the Roman head as the head of a Muruṇḍa king; he has missed to notice the loop attached to the piece (*op. cit.,* p. 135, fn. 3).
17. *J.N.S.I.,* pp. 73-81; infra pp. 103-112.
18. *J.B.O.R.S.,* V, p. 233.
19. These were first published by S.V. Sohoni (*I.N.C.,* I. p. 86). He identified the Gupta coin as that of Candragupta II and the other coin as of Vāsudeva with doubt. Later R.K. Chaudhury republished them (*I.N.C.,* II, p. 84). He correctly attributed the Gupta coin to Samudragupta but then he thought that the other coin possibly belongs to Huviṣka. Perhaps he was not aware that Huviṣka never used standing king motif for his gold coins. The coin has a trident on the left, feature of post-Vāsudeva coins. S.P. Singh has followed the wrong attribution of Chaudhury and has also missed to notice that these coins were looped.
20. *P.J.A.S.B.,* 1885, p. 129.
21. These coins were deposited in the Patna Museum (Coin Register Nos. 2091-92) but were subsequently lost in a theft. However, they are described in some detail in the Coin-Register. On its basis Altekar has published these coins (*J.N.S.I.,* XIII, p. 146). In the Museum Register both the coins are attributed to Vāsudeva. But, as has been pointed out by Altekar, one coin did not have any portion of the name which could be read as BAZODEO; and no coin of Vāsudeva is known with Ardokṣo reverse. This may, therefore, be a coin of Kaniṣka III. S.P. Singh has missed to notice this find.
22. Information based on the Treasure Trove Report in the Patna Museum. The coins were lost subsequently in a theft in the Patna Museum; so the reading of the letters on the right cannot be testified.
23. *I.N.C.,* II, p. 84, Pl. II. The note is confusing in respect of the Kuṣāṇa coins; the coins are not clearly attributed to any king there; but the illustrations are captioned as the coins of Kaniṣka. The author does not seem to be conversant with the Kuṣāṇa gold coins. The Standing King--Oeṣo type coin has clearly a trident on the left on the obverse; and this shows that it was a post-Vāsudeva coin. The published rubbings do not show the legend, which is probably truncated; but if the legend read by the author is correct, then it may be attributed to Kaniṣka III. The other coin may at a glance be attributed to Huviṣka by the simple fact that the obverse bears a bust.
24. *J.P.A.S.B.,* XXVIII, 1932, pp. 127ff. Pl. I. 1 and 3. S.P. Singh mentions only

one coin (Coin 1); but most likely he refers to second coin (Coin 3) without mentioning the place-name and said that it is an imitation gold coin of Kuṣāṇa type (*op. cit.*, p. 134, fn. 5).

25. *J.P.A.S.B.*, XXVIII, 1932, pp. 127ff, Pl. I, No. 2.
26. *P.A.S.B.*, 1890, p. 162.
27. *Gauḍarājamālā* (Bengali), p. 4. This reference is given by S.P. Singh for an imitation coin of Vāsudeva in base gold (*op. cit.*, p. 134, fn. 5).
28. *J.N.S.I.*, XVII, p. 109; *Inventory of the Hoards and find of Coins and Seals from Madhya Pradesh*, p. 9.
29. *A.S.I.,A.R.*, 1918-19, pp. 46ff.
30. Unpublished. Personal information.
31. Unpublished. Personal information.
32. *A.S.I.,A.R.*, 1935-36, p. 64.
33. *Ibid.*, 1936-37, pp. 49-55.
34. Information contained in the Treasure Trove Report with the Patna Museum. There the Kuṣāṇa imitation coins are mentioned as Purī-Kuṣāṇa, but the actual coins in the Museum show that it was an imitation of the Punjab type and not Purī-Kuṣāṇa.
35. Personal information.
36. K.P. Jayaswal, Presidential Address, Numismatic Society of India, 1936, *Sixty Years of the Numismatic Society of India*, p. 1.
37. Only seven of these coins are mentioned by S.P. Singh (*op. cit.*, p. 130) on the basis of the information contained in the published list (*I.N.C.*, VIII, p. 53, No. 25).
38. *A.S.I.,A.R.*, 1913-14, p. 181.
39. *Vaiśālī Excavations*, 1958-62, pp. 132, 149ff.
40. S.R. Roy, *A Guide to Vaiśālī Museum*, pp. 16ff.
41. *Annual Report of K.P. Jayaswal Research Institute*, 1961, p. 4.
42. *J.N.S.I.*, XIII, pp. 121ff.
43. *A.S.I.,A.R.*, 1912-13, pp. 84ff.
44. *Ibid.*, (*Eastern Circle*), 1913-14, p. 74.
45. *J.N.S.I.*, XIII, pp. 144ff.
46. *Kumrahar Excavations*, 1951-55, p. 99.
47. Unpublished. Indian Museum Register No. 6491. Mentioned by S.P. Singh (*op. cit.*, p. 134).
48. *I.C.*, III, p. 727.
49. *J.N.S.I.*, II, p. 124.

50. Treasure Trove Report (*I.N.C.,* List No. 81).
51. *J.B.O.R.S.,* V, p. 78, fn. 2.
52. Treasure Trove Report (List No. 225).
53. *Ibid.,* (List No. 229).
54. *Ibid.,* (List No. 12).
55. *J.B.O.R.S.,* V, pp. 73ff.
56. *A.S.I.,A.R.,* 1624-25, p. 130.
57. *Ancient India,* No. 5, p. 97.
58. Treasure Trove Report (*I.N.C.,* VI, No. 4).
59. *O.H.R.J.,* II, pp. 84-93.
60. *M.J.L.S.,* 1858, pp. 75-78.
61. *C.A.S.R.,* XIII, p. 116.
62. *J.N.S.I.,* II, p. 124.
63. *O.H.R.J.,* II, p. 85.
64. *J.N.S.I.,* XIII, p. 69.
65. *A.S.I.,A.R.,* 1924-25, pp. 131-32.
66. *I.N.C.,* VI, p. 79; T.T. No. 13. The information contained herein seems to be incomplete. The hoard also contained some coins of Kaniṣka and Huviṣka (*B.M.C.,A.I.,* intro., p. cxxi).
67. *Ibid.,* intro. p. cxxi.
68. *O.H.R.J.,* II, p. 85.
69. *J.N.S.I.,* IX, p. 107.
70. *Ibid.,* II, p. 124.
71. *History of Orissa,* I, pp. 111-15.
72. *P.A.S.B.* 1895, pp. 61-65.
73. *Ibid.*
74. *J.N.S.I.,* XXXII, pp. 25ff.
75. T.T. No. 3 of 1922-23; *J.N.S.I.,* XVII, p. 109; *Inventory of the Hoards and finds of Coins and Seals from Madhya Pradesh,* p. 9.
76. *Ibid.,* p. 109; *Ibid.,* p. 10.
77. *Ibid.,* p. 109; *Ibid.,* p. 10.
78. *Ibid.,* p. 109, *Ibid.,* p. 9.
79. *J.N.S.I.,* XXVII, pp. 118-19; XXVIII, pp. 1-3.
80. Information supplied by M.K. Hussain of the Directorate of Archaeology, Maharashtra, Bombay.
81. *P.A.S.B.,* 1882, p. 113.

82. *The Age of the Kuṣāṇas,* p. 238 fn. 42.
83. *Buddhist Antiquities of Nagarjunikonda,* pp. 21-22.
84. *Ancient India,* No. 5, p. 101; Pl. Lb.
85. *J.N.S.I.,* III, Pl. V. 17-19.
86. Unpublished in Allahabad Museum.
87. *Report of the Archaeological Department, Gwalior State, 1938-39,* p. 18, Pl. XXVIIIb; *J.N.S.I.,* XXXII, p. 201.
88. *Explorations at Karad,* p. 30, Pl. XIV, c-d.
89. *Excavations at Brahmapuri* 1945-46, Pl. XXVIB, 6.
90. *Excavations at Bhokardan,* 1973, pp. 74-76.
91. *A.B.O.R.I.,* XXII, pp. 179-80, Pl. XIIIb.
92. *Supplement to the Annual Report of the Mysore Archaeological Department* 1929, p. 29.
93. *I.A.,* II, p. 213.
94. *Catalogue of Venetian Coins in the Madras Government Museum,* pp. 4-5.
95. Unpublished. They were seen by me, when I was Numismatist there.
96. *Catalogue of Venetian Coins,* p. 4.
97. *J.N.S.I.,* XIII, p. 146.
98. *Ibid.* XX, p. 3.
99. S.P. Singh suggests the prevalence of Kuṣāṇa gold currency in the deltaic region of Bengal introduced during the reign of Kaniṣka on the basis of the mention of the gold coin called *Caltis* in the *Periplus of the Erythrean Sea.* But gold coins of Kaniṣka or Huviṣka are yet to be found there.
100. *J.N.S.I.,* XII, pp. 121-23; XIII, pp. 144-47; XX, pp. 1-3.
101. *Ibid.,* XIII, pp. 107ff; *I.H.Q.,* XXVII, pp. 294-303.
102. *Ibid.,* XXXV, pp. 127ff.
103. *History of Orissa,* I, pp. 115ff.
104. *J.N.S.I.,* XXVIII, pp. 6-11.
105. *Ibid.,* XXXII, pp. 25ff.
106. *Ibid.,* XXVIII, pp. 1-3.
107. The belief that the find-spots of copper coins are good evidence of rule, because they do not travel far from the place of issue, is unfounded. Copper coins must have circulated regularly over all the country served by the mint of issue, which might be very extensive, and a good deal more than that can be determined. (Tarn, *The Greeks in Bactria and India,* p. 441).

108. *Cambirdge History of India*, I (Delhi, 1955) p. 162. Also see *Buddhist India*, (Calcutta, 1957), p. 12.
109. *Ancient Geography of India*, p. 518.
110. Altekar thinks that the Mitra kings of Ayodhyā who issued the Bull and Cock type coins, were *most probably* slightly later than the time of Kaniṣka or Vāsudeva. He places them in the second century A.D. and suggests that they *probably* ruled as feudatories of the Kuṣāṇas and were allowed to issue coins (*J.N.S.I.*, XII, p. 123). But the suggestion holds no validity, if we realise the fact that the Guptas and Mughals were the two great dynasties of India; but none of them ever allowed any of their feudatories to issue their own coins. Altekar himself has admitted that no Gupta feudatory was ever permitted to mint any coins (*The Guptas-Vākāṭaka Age*, p. 41, fn. 2). I wonder on what ground then he had placed this suggestion. Had Kuṣāṇas any feudatories at Ayodhyā and permitted them to issue their own coins their coins would have been certainly influenced by the Kuṣāṇa coinage but the Ayodhyā coins are entirely free from any such influence. This certainly indicates that they were entirely independent.
111. *J.N.S.I.*, XX, pp. 4-5; *I.H.Q.*, XXIX, p. 216.
112. This later date is now being suggested by many scholars. Different views on this point were expressed at a Seminar held at London. *Papers on the Date of Kaniṣka*, Leiden.
113. I, myself had not been immune of such belief. I have very much relied on this theory in a number of papers published earlier. But I was not correct. These papers need careful review in the light of what is being said here.
114. S.P. Singh (*op. cit.*, pp. 127ff). The idea, was originally mooted by D.K. Ganguly (*J.N.S.I.*, XXVIII, p. 11).
115. *J.B.O.R.S.*, V, p. 180.
116. *B.M.C.,A.I.*, intro. p. cxii, fn. 2.
117. *J.N.S.I.*, XIII, p. 69.
118. *Ancient India*, No. 5, p. 97.
119. Smith had dated the Purī-Kuṣāṇa coins on his own considerations in the fourth-fifth century A.D. (*I.M.C.*, I, pp. 64-65). P. Acharya has suggested that the Purī-Kuṣāṇa coins represent the kings of Orissa who flourished in the Gupta period (*J.N.S.I.*, II, pp. 125-26).
120. This study is expected to be published under the title *Early Indian Copper Artefacts*.
121. Route map in Author's Doctoral Thesis entitled *Punch Marked Coins of Ancient India*, submitted to Benaras Hindu University (Unpublished).
122. *I.N.C.* VI.i, p. 51.

123. P.L. Gupta, *Roman Coins from Andhra Pradesh,* Haiderabad, 1965.
124. *J.N.S.I.,* XXIX, pp. 19ff.
125. *Ibid.,* XII, p. 81.
126. Coins in Colombo Museum, collected in the Island.
127. *Indian Antiquary,* XXXIII, pp. 217ff.
128. A number of the Central Asian finds of such counterstruck coins of the Kuṣāṇas are listed in the Numismatic Section of the *Annotated Bibliography of Soviet Central Asian Archaeology and the Kuṣāṇa Culture,* published on the occasion of the International Conference on the History, Archaeology and Culture of Central Asia in Kuṣāṇa period, held in 1968 at Dushambe.
129. The numismatic evidence being thus negative, there is no point in discussing the evidences of epigraphy and art, which by themselves are flimsy. No inscription bearing the name of Kaniṣka or Huviṣka has been found in any part of Eastern India beyond Vārāṇasī. The few inscriptions cited by Adris Banerji were in the script, which has been called 'Kuṣāṇa' by the epigraphists for convenience. This does not mean that it was the exclusive script of Kuṣāṇa rulers. It only means that the inscriptions were inscribed in the period, when Kuṣāṇas were ruling in the country and the script was in vogue in that period. Likewise the few stone sculptures, that are identified as Kuṣāṇa, found in these regions, are made of red sandstone of Karrā and thus are the products imported from Mathura. They mean nothing in the present context. The terracotta figurines, to which reliance is made by some scholars to suggest the Kuṣāṇa domination in Bihar etc., are actually very much similar to those that are found at many places in Uttar Pradesh. They cannot be distinguished as local product of any place if mixed with those of the Uttar Pradesh finds. So they may not necessarily be local products. Even today, the terracotta figurines of Gaṇeśa and Lakṣmī, which are in demand during Dīpāvalī, are imported to Patna and many other places in Bihar from Vārāṇasī. Even if the terracotta figurines be the local products of Bihar, they bear testimony only to cultural contacts of the people and do not have any political meaning.
130. The gold coins were equally profuse in the time of the Mughal emperors; but we know from Tavernier who visited India five times between 1641 and 1666, that the gold coins were not current among the merchants. They were scarcely ever to be met with save the houses of the great nobles (*Travels,* Ed. Ball, I, p. 18). Thevenot, another traveller of the same period, also testifies the same fact. He writes that the gold coins pass not commonly in trade (*Travels,* English Translation 1687, part III, p. 18). The same would have been true in the time of the Guptas.

7

Romano-Kuṣāṇa Medallion
Nature and Importance*

In 1972, when I was for some time with the Department of Coins and Medals in the British Museum, its keeper G.K. Jenkins showed me an unusual gold medallion having a central circular disc, mounted with a broad border of several rope and bead strings with an ear on the top (*fig. 29*). The object, thus, is in the nature of a jewellery and it was meant to be used as a pendant of a necklace or some other ornament. Its numismatic interest lies in the circular disc, which bears the bust of the Roman Emperor Constantine I on one side and the Kuṣāṇa goddess Ardokṣo (standing, as seen on the coins of Huviṣka). This unusual coupling of a typical Roman type with a typical Kuṣāṇa type had attracted the attention of R. Göbl long before me; and he published a note about it in a German Numismatic Journal.[1]

In his Note, Göbl has traced out the origin of the Roman motif in those coins that were issued during 325-326 A.D. at the *Vicennalia* of Constantine and Nicaenum. He has also noticed similarity between the Kuṣāṇa enthroned Ardokṣo, seen on some Vāsudeva coins and the enthroned figure of Constantinopolis on the silver medallions issued in 330 A.D. On the basis of this similarity, he postulated that had this form (i.e., enthroned) of Ardokṣo been known to the imitator, he would have naturally taken it as his model; since he did not, according to him, it meant

* Originally published in *Journal of the Numismatic Society of India*, XXXVIII (1976), pp. 73-81.

that the present medallion was not produced long after 325 A.D. Consequently, he is of the opinion that the reigns of the Kuṣāṇa king Huviṣka and Constantine the Great cannot have been widely separated in time. In conclusion he suggests, "While the Sassanians were striving to take the Kuṣāṇa empire between pincers with the help of the Guptas, Rome, under Constantine, recognised the Kuṣāṇas as a distant opponent of the Sassanians, with whom it might attempt in its turn to involve the Persian Empire in a war on two fronts. It is thus possible that *Vicennalia* issues of various kinds were sent to the Kuṣāṇa court and the mixed medallion owes its origin to this occurrence."

This curious medallion was re-published by Göbl in the *Journal of the Numismatic Society of India*.[2] While he has reiterated his earlier views about the prototypes of the two sides of the central disc of the medallion with some more details, his conclusions here are very much different. Now he said that (i) it was struck in India; (ii) it was the product of a normal Kuṣāṇa mint; (iii) it would have been issued either within the space about 325 and 330 A.D. or only shortly later (not in any case later than 337 A.D.); it was issued by Vāsudeva II. The reason for issuing this mixed-type piece, given by him, is entirely new. He now says, "Vāsudeva was looking for political help in the struggle with Kaniṣka II to the old friends of his father Huviṣka. Since the emperor, to whose help he appealed was Constantine I himself, as shown by the obverse, the medallion should be, in any case, issued before 337 A.D., the year of the death of the great monarch." With these assumptions, Göbl considered this piece as an important testimony for (i) the relation of the Later Imperial Rome and the Kuṣāṇa State in India; and (ii) the Kuṣāṇa chronology.

One may very well agree with Göbl so far as the identity of the bust of Constantine I, depicted on the piece, is concerned. It might well have been imitated from those coins that he has cited as its proto-type; and on its basis it may be said that the piece could not have been produced at any date earlier than 325 A.D. This may be *terminus ante quem*. But no *terminus post quem* may be fixed. It is extremely difficult to agree with him that its production was confined to the period between 325 and 337 A.D. on the evidence adduced by him. The suggestion that the enthroned figure of Constantinopolis was the prototype of enthroned Ardokṣo, seen on the coins of Kaniṣka III (Göbl's Kaniṣka II) is merely hypothetical. It is based on his assumption that the Kaniṣka era began in 232 A.D.[3] This date cannot be used for any purpose till it is firmly established.

If this date 232 A.D. is admitted for the beginning of the era, it may be pointed out that Zeus enthroned could be the prototype for the enthroned Ardokṣo to be adopted on the Kuṣāṇa coinage. Zeus enthroned was a very common motif on the Indo-Greek coins and is seen as late as the last ruler of the race — Hermeus.[4] Not only that, it is also found on some of the Śaka-Pahlava coins.[5] The Indo-Greek and Śaka-Pahlava coins have often been found along with the Kuṣāṇa coins. As such, it was much more readily available to the Kuṣāṇa mint-masters for adoption than the Roman commemorative pieces of Constantinople having the enthroned Constantinopolis, which were rare and are never known in the territories of the Kuṣāṇas.

In spite of this, even if we assume that the motifs on the two sides of the piece were contemporary, as suggested by Göbl, we must be sure about the purposeful and convincing motive behind the issue of the piece with motifs belonging to two entirely different states, situated widely apart. We do know of trade relations between the distant Rome and the Kuṣāṇa kingdom; but we do not have even the slightest indication anywhere in archaeology or history of any political or diplomatic relations between the two. We have nothing to say that Constantine I or any other Roman emperor had any kind of friendship with Huviṣka or any other Kuṣāṇa ruler. In the absence of any such basic evidence, the explanations suggested by Göbl for the issue of this piece in his German Note as well as in the Indian article would remain simply an imagination having no meaning and carrying no weight.

Sassanids had snatched the western part of the Kuṣāṇa kingdom and they claimed for themselves, the overlordship over the Kuṣāṇas or the Kuṣāṇa territories; but we do not know from any source that the Guptas had ever exerted any pressure against the Kuṣāṇas, in whatsoever manner. Even if we presume, in the tune of Göbl, that the Kuṣāṇas were in between the pincers of the Sassanids and the Guptas, we are not aware of any Roman and Sassanid conflict, that had ever taken place, nor we have heard of any idea having occurred in the minds of any Roman emperor to attack the Sassanid territories. If any such possibility could be postulated for any reason, only then in the light of the political theory that 'enemy's enemy is a good friend', it may be said that the Kuṣāṇas and the Romans might have been good friends and would have come into some alliance against their common enemy, the Sassanids. This might be the idea behind Göbl's suggestion. But if the conditions be viewed from the practical point, it may be easily realised that the Roman emperor could not have any kind of expectations from the Kuṣāṇas in case of any Roman-Sassanid war; and equally there was no chance for the Kuṣāṇas to extend their hands of friendship to the Roman emperor against the Sassanids.

In any Roman-Sassanid war, the Kuṣāṇas, at their best, could only have put some pressure from their side on the Sassanid territory to ease the situation on the other side in favour of the Romans. But this would have been suicidal for themselves. They were no match to the Sassanid power. Any pressure from the side of the Kuṣāṇas over the Sassanid territory would have served no purpose in favour of the Romans; rather, it would have brought a fresh wrath for themselves from the Sassanids, whose victim they already were. Göbl has himself admitted that the Kuṣāṇas were sandwiched between the pressures of the Sassanids and the Guptas. In the moment of such a pressure, the Kuṣāṇas, having the Sassanids entangled in a war with an equally powerful enemy, would have taken a sigh of some relief; and it would have been in their best interest to keep themselves aloof from that war. They would have never shown any gesture of friendship towards Rome. In view of these simple facts, in case of any Roman-Sassanid clash, any gift from the Roman emperor to the Kuṣāṇa court would have never brought any desired result. The Roman

Emperor Constantine I would not have been so fool as to send gifts of the *Vicennalia* issues of various kinds to appease the Kuṣāṇa monarch by issuing the hybrid piece for no material gain.

Even if we go to the extent of the absurd presumption that Constantine I was idiot and he could not assess the correct political situation and was foolish enough to issue the piece for appeasing the Kuṣāṇa monarch in some false hope, the medallion itself does not favours any such presumption; nor it suggests that it was the product of any Roman mint.

Had the piece been a product of any Roman mint, the cutters of its dies would have never blundered or barbarised the Roman legend, with which they were so familiar and which they were daily cutting in the dies for the coins of their own mint. Again, the persons, responsible for the production of the piece would not have been unaware about the purpose for which it was being produced. They would have undoubtedly known that the piece was meant for Huviṣka to appease him and that it was an invitation for a war-alliance or at least for a diplomatic friendship. They would have never selected Ardokṣo for the piece, who was the goddess of wealth and prosperity and not of war, victory or friendship. There was no dearth of gods and goddesses in the realm of Huviṣka's coinage, who could carry the message aptly. The inappropriate selection of the Goddess is, by itself, another indication that the piece was never meant for the purpose suggested. Had the piece been meant to be sent as gift to Huviṣka the die-cutters would have certainly taken every care to reproduce the *tamghā,* the personal insignia of Huviṣka, correctly. They would have certainly not missed even one horizontal bar, as we find in the piece, as the *tamghā* is always found prominently on the Kuṣāṇa coins and could never be missed even by a layman's eyes, what to say of those who were meant to see the coins.

It seems that Göbl has realised the absurdity of his suggestion placed in the German note; and most likely for this reason, he has abandoned it in his latest article and has propounded a new theory to explain the piece. But unfortunately his new theory is equally baseless and untenable.

There is no evidence whatsoever to suggest that Vāsudeva II had any struggle with Kaniṣka II (or III). The numismatic evidences are clear enough to show that the succession from Vāsudeva II to Kaniṣka III (Göbl's K̃aniṣka II) was peaceful and smooth. Vāsudeva II had no occasion to seek any political or military assistance from any quarter. Even if he would have had any such necessity, it is unlikely that he would have looked towards Rome and sought assistance from Constantine I in spite of his friendly relations (of which we have no evidence) with Huviṣka. It was physically impossible for Rome and its emperor to come to the rescue of Vāsudeva II without endangering his own position with the intervening kingdom of the Sassanids. Even if we believe that Vāsudeva II looked towards Constantine I for help and had to issue any special medallion to meet this end, it would go without saying that he would have had his own identity disclosed on it along with that of the Roman Emperor. On the present medallion, while we have the bust of his ally the Roman Emperor, copied on one side, we have nothing on the other side, which could be said Vāsudeva II's own. If nothing else, at least his personal *tamghā* should have been there; but even that is absent. Instead, here is the figure of Ardokṣo, borrowed from Huviṣka's coins; and that too, was such a motif that does not befit the occasion. If this motif was meant on the medallion to stress the friendship of Huviṣka with the Roman Emperor, as Göbl seems to suggest, a suitable motif could have been conveniently selected from amongst the gods and goddesses, known on the coins of Huviṣka, who could have symbolised friendship, peace, war or victory. The goddess in dress, anatomy and sculptural style is conspicuously unlike any Kuṣāṇa version. The drapery has a peculiarly fluid, unoccupied look. Anatomical carelessness is so marked that one cannot be sure whether it is the right arm that supports the cornucopiae or it is merely the bottom of pepulam. The entire motif is absolutely un-Kuṣāṇian. These facts create doubt about the medallion having been issued by Vāsudeva II or any other Kuṣāṇa ruler for the purpose suggested by Göbl. That the medallion was decidedly not issued by any Kuṣāṇa ruler is apparent from the facts that the *tamghā* on it is defective and the legend *Ardokṣo* is not correctly reproduced. It is unthinkable that any Kuṣāṇa engraver would have been so stupid as not to know their correct forms and commit such glaring mistakes.

To sum up, there is nothing in the medallion that could make one believe that it was the product of any Roman mint (as was impliedly suggested by Göbl in his German Note) or of a Kuṣāṇa mint (as is openly declared by him in his later article) and is testimony of any (real or fictitious) political or diplomatic relations between Rome and the Kuṣāṇa State of India. There is also nothing in it to show, in any way, that the two motifs, adopted on the two sides, were borrowed from two contemporary coins and that they suggest any contemporaneity between Constantine I and Huviṣka or Vāsudeva II and that it was an unimpeachable evidence to support the date of Kaniṣka era, propounded by Göbl. *Prima facie*, the medallion is nothing more than a fantasy, a creation of some fanciful jeweller. It has no worth for history.

The medallion may, however, be interesting from numismatist's point of view and one might like to know the source of this fanciful piece. In the context discussed above, Göbl in his later paper has thought of its Indian origin. Coins undoubtedly have fascinated Indian people and they used coins for necklaces, bracelets or pendants. Kuṣāṇa coins were not new to those who were accustomed to use coins as jewellery.[6] Roman coins have also attracted Indians for this purpose. They used not only the original Roman coins but also manufactured clay bullae with Roman heads or busts.[7] A gold piece is also known which, like the present medallion, has a Kuṣāṇa coin motif on one side and a Roman motif on the other.[8] Göbl has cited this piece in his paper. But such Indian imitations of Roman coins are always crude and barbarous in their execution and none of them bears any likeness with the head or bust of any particular Roman emperor. The Indians were unconcerned about the real portrait. A comparison of the present medallion with the Indian imitations would show that the former depicts not only a true bust of

Constantine I, but its fabric and execution is fine and un-Indian. Moreover, the coins or their imitations, that were used in Indian jewellery, never had any mounting frame as seen in the present medallion. They used only an ear at the top without any decorative mounting. Thus this medallion is quite different in its form; this makes it almost certain that the medallion did not originate in India.

Its un-Indian origin is also suggested by the fact that it came to the Coin Department of the British Museum from its Roman Department.[9] Had it come from any Indian source, it would have reached as an Indian jewellery to the Department of Oriental Art or as coin would have come direct to the Coin Department. Hence there is every likelihood that it came to the Museum from some European source and from European country.

But we need not be presumptive on this point. While coming back from London, I stopped at Munster (Germany) for a lecture at the University. There, in the office of Peter Berghaus, the Director of the local Museum, I saw an enlarged photograph of a gold medallion which, like the British Museum medallion, had a central disc with the portrait of a Roman emperor surrounded by a broad frame of several zig-zag patterns and an ear at the top (*fig. 30*). This medallion and the British Museum medallion both carry the same pattern. The two differ only in their technical details. In the British Museum medallion the frame was made separately and was soldered to the central disc; here the central disc and the frame both were struck as one die. The basic pattern being the same, it is quite clear that the two medallions were manufactured for the same people, who had liking for Roman coin motifs and preferred a broad frame around it.

On enquiry, I was told that the medallion, of which the photograph I had seen in Berghaus' room, was found in Sweden at Senorn, Torn, Ramdale Parish, Blekinge province in 1936 and is deposited in the Statens Historika Museum, Stockholm, and was published in 1952.[10] In the opinion of John Kent of the British Museum, whom the photograph of the medallion was shown,[11] the bust is based on that of Constantine II (336-360 A.D.) as depicted on gold *solidi* and on large medallions to the value of nine *solidi*. The portrait has, however, been reversed by the engraver and faces left instead of right.[12] In Berghaus' opinion, it might have been made in Scandinavia in the fifth century A.D.[13] The same may be true about the British Museum medallion.

Göbl himself has admitted in his paper that the frame of the British Museum medallion has many western parallels that date from the time of the Roman emperor Honorius (393-423 A.D.). He also admits that the polygonal ear and its art was typical of the fifth century A.D.[14] As such, according to Göbl's own admission, the frame dates not earlier than the fifth century. He laid aside this evidence and took no notice of the frame as it was against his own imaginations about the central disc. If we do not ignore the frame and the ear, as Göbl did, anyone, who holds no pre-notions about the central disc, would unhesitatingly admit that the two — the disc and the frame with ear — were the art of one and the same period and were the works of the same jeweller-artist.

The reverse motif, the standing Ardokṣo adopted from the coins of Huviṣka, is in no way a bar to the identification of the medallion as of Scandinavian or Western European origin. It is well-known that the Kuṣāṇa coins have been found in western and northern Europe.[15] One of those Kuṣāṇa coins might have caught the fascination of someone somewhere only in Europe, in the same way as the Roman coins fascinated the Indians, and he or she got its copy placed on the reverse of the medallion.[16] If this medallion has got any value for us, it is only that it may be an evidence of the extension of the Kuṣāṇa coins in Europe and perhaps also of the trade relations with India, direct or indirect.

References

1. Zwei neur Termini fur ein Zentrales, Datum der Alten Geschichte Mittelasiens, das Jahr I des Kuṣāṇkonigs Kaniṣka, In *Anzeiger der phil-list. Klasse der Osterreicheschen Akademie der Wissenschaften,* Jahrgang 1964, So. 7, pp. 149-51. English translation of this note was provided to me by my good friend N. W. Lowick of the British Museum.

2. *J.N.S.I.,* XXXVIII, I, pp. 21-26.
3. No scholar shares his views about this date.
4. A. N. Lahiri, *Corpus of Indo-Greek Coins,* Pl. III. 3; IV. 2, 3, 7; V., 3. 4, XXI, 1, 2, 5, 9, etc.
5. *P.M.C.,* Indo-Greek Coins, Pl. XV. i.
6. *J.N.S.I.,* XXXVI, pp. 30-31; XXXVII, pp. 76ff.
7. Finds of Roman clay bullae are listed by the author in *J.N.S.I.,* XXXVI, p. 39; supra, p. 52.
8. *J.N.S.I.,* XII, pp. 1-4; *Ancient India,* No. 5, p. 97.
9. Mentioned by Göbl in his paper in *J.N.S.I.,* XXXVIII, p. 22.
10. *Mackepranqe – De Nordiske Guldbrakteater,* p. 159. Berghaus has also published a note about it; *Bodenaltertumer Westfalens,* XII, p. 72. Pl. 18. 10.
11. N.W. Lowick has kindly taken trouble to consult him on my behalf and his views were conveyed to me in the letter dated 17th March 1975.
12. The portrait may be of Valentine II (375-395 A.D.) according to another scholar.
13. Personal letter to the author dated 29th October 1974.
14. *J.N.S.I.,* XXXVIII, p. 23.
15. B. Gufurov, *Kuṣāṇa Civilization and World Culture,* 1968, p. 11.
16. Alexender C. Soper has discussed the medallion in quite detail; he thinks that it may be a modern forgery. Altrnatively, he suggests that a wealthy patron of some third nationality – an Armenian merchant prince, might have ordered the piece as a kind of talisman or thanks-offering, recording his debt to two powers, an East Roman emperor and as east Iranian goddess of good fortune. A skilful native die-cutter with a coin of Constantine to copy, but perhaps only a description of the goddess, to whom both Latin and Greek were wholly alien scripts, might have prepared it. He further adds that this medallion could ever be made truly relevant to the date of Kaniṣka is beyond his power of belief. (*Artibus Asiae,* XXXIV, p. 113).

8

Chronology of Post-Vāsudeva Rulers and Allied Tribes*

THE Kuṣāṇas are known to have an extensive empire stretched from the Yamuno-Gaṅgā plains in the east to Afghanistan and Central Asia in the west. This extensive empire crumbled during or after the death of Vāsudeva. This downfall of the Kuṣāṇa empire is generally attributed to the invasion of the Sassanids, who founded a powerful kingdom in Persia. The Sassanids occupied the Kuṣāṇa territories only west of Indus; if they penetrated deep into India, east of Indus, is not known from any source.

No power within India, during this period is known, who could claim the overthrow of the Kuṣāṇas from the Indian soil. It is suggested by some historians[1] that the Yaudheyas and the Nāgas might have ousted the Kuṣāṇas from the Mathura region. But this suggestion is merely speculative and has no basic foundation. Even if it be true, there is no evidence to show that the Nāgas had ever extended their kingdom beyond Padmāvatī (or Mathura). The Yaudheyas were ousted by the Western Kṣatrapas from their colonial home in Rajasthan; and they had taken shelter in a corner of Haryana in or about this period is known from their coins.[2] As such, even if they had succeeded in over-powering the Kuṣāṇas in the Mathura region, they could never have been able to drive out the Kuṣāṇas from the entire Indian soil.

---

* Originally published in *K.P. Jayaswal Commemoration Volume,* Patna, 1981, pp. 291-299.

Kuṣāṇas existed in India at least up to the time of Samudragupta is well attested from the Allahabad Pillar inscription, where *Daivaputra-ṣāhi-ṣāhānuṣāhi* and *Ṣaka-muruṇḍa* are mentioned as existing on the borderland of the Gupta empire.[3]

The history of the post-Vāsudeva Kuṣāṇas or, to be more precise, the history of Northern India till the rise of the Guptas in the Yamuno-Gaṅgā plains, is in considerable obscurity. We get a clear picture of political history from this time onward for the mid-northern India (*Madhyadeśa*); but the historical facade of the North-Western India (i.e., the region which is now covered by Pakistan and the two States of India — Punjab and Haryana) still remains shrouded with mist.

No contemporary inscription or any other reliable archaeological evidence is available to throw light upon the events of this period. What we have of this period relating to the later Kuṣāṇas (post-Vāsudeva Kuṣāṇas) and the allied tribes, are their coins. They bear out names of their issuers; and are helpful only in drawing an outline of the history of the period. But even this material has not yet been properly worked out for the history.

This series of the post-Vāsudeva coinage had its origin in the coins of Vāsudeva himself. The gold coins of Vāsudeva are of the similar fabric as those issued by his predecessors -- Kaniṣka and Huviṣka. They display the same type: the standing king extending his right hand to the fire-altar on the obverse and Śiva standing in front of the bull, with the legend *Oeṣo* on the reverse. These coins are almost always well struck and neatly engraved and they bear the inscription carefully engraved and accurate. The obverse field is clear and bears no symbol. From this type of coins, emerged two distinct series of the coinage in two different areas. One series was issued by the early Sassanid conquerors and their governors and is found confined to the west of Indus. With this series we are not concerned here.

The other series was that which is known mostly in the area considerably to the east of Indus and was issued by

Vāsudeva's successors and the chiefs of the Tribal Kuṣāṇas that followed them. These coins may be isolated into five well defined types, based on their fabric and contents. They may fairly be arranged in a chronological order:

(i) Very similar to the coins of Vāsudeva in type and inscriptions but different in style. Here is a Brāhmī letter *ha* in the right obverse field. This may well be taken to be the issue of the successor of Vāsudeva, who succeeded him immediately after his death. Since the circular legend discloses no other name than Vāsudeva, it is reasonable to presume that this successor also had the same name Vāsudeva. He may well be designated as Vāsudeva II. A notable point about these coins is that the Brāhmī letter *ha* was not exclusively used on the obverse; it is sometimes seen on the reverse also. Then, there are other coins of this variety, where letters other than *ha* are used; and at times, these letters are seen at three places in the field. Besides the right field, they are also seen in the left and the central field. If they mean something different than what a single letter meant is difficult to say; but it may be said that this use is a later development, which was followed in the subsequent varieties.

(ii) Same as the coins of variety (i) with the Brāhmī letters invariably at three places in the obverse field — left, centre and right. The difference in the coins of this variety from the variety (i) lies in the fact that it bears the obverse circular legend as *Ṣāo Nāno Ṣāo Kaneṣko Koṣāno* in place of *Ṣāo Nāno Ṣāo Bazodeo Koṣāno*. This new legend by itself declares that the coins were issued by a king named Kaniṣka. This Kaniṣka may be designated as Kaniṣka III.

(iii) Same as var. (ii) so far the obverse is concerned; and as such may be the coinage of Kaniṣka III; but it has a quite different reverse. Here is a new device of a sitting goddess on a high-backed throne with the name *Ardokṣo*. This variety was the prototype for the subsequent varieties and it was later adopted on the Gupta coins. Besides this major change, this variety has another peculiarity. While in the earlier varieties (i) and (ii) single Brāhmī letter is noticed at all the three places of the obverse field, here in the right field the single Brāhmī letter is replaced by a syllable or word of at least two letters like *Vasu, Vīru, Mahī,* which appear to be part of personal names. These might be the names of successive or subordinate rulers; but this is just a guess.

(iv) Same as the *Ardokṣo* type coins; but the circular Graeco-Bactrian legend of the time of Vāsudeva and Kaniṣka III is replaced by cursive Kuṣāṇo-Bactrian script, similar to that which is seen on the Kuṣāṇo-Sassanian coins. It apparently looks like the repetition of 0000; and for this reason it has been declared by Cunningham as illegible.[4] Its cursive Kuṣāṇo-Bactrian nature is suggested here for the first time. It is now for the paleographists, who know this script, to confirm or reject the suggestion. However, the form of the legend by itself suggests that this variety was issued by a quite different branch of rulers. On these coins, outside the spear, i.e., in the right field, are found a word of two, three or four Brāhmī letters that form a word. These words have been read as *Ṣaka, Ṣālad, Gaḍahara* or *Gaḍakhara.* They are considered to be the tribal names. In the central field, i.e., below the arm of the king, are also the words or syllables. For instance, on the coins bearing the right legend *Ṣaka* has the word below the king's arm as *Sita* or *Saya.* Likewise, the coins bearing the word *Ṣālada* have the word as *Bhadra* and those having *Gaḍahara* have the word *Samudra, Kīrada* etc. These all appear to be proper names; but to whom they meant is difficult to say.

(v) Same as the *Ardokṣo* type of coins with circular legends most likely as on type (iv) but mostly cut or out of flank. Here the obverse Brāhmī inscriptions that are seen on the above types in the left and right field are eliminated; only below the arm of the king it is retained and is read as *Kida* or *Kidāra.* It is understood that they stand for the Kidarites. On the reverse of these coins, we have for first time the Brāhmī legend representing personal proper names in place of the name of the goddess in Greek. The names that are found on the reverse have been read as *Śrī Ṣāhi, Kidāra, Kṛtavīrya, Sarvayaśasa, Bhāsvan, Śīlāditya, Prakāśa, Kuśala, Saloṇavīra* etc. Here we may definitely say that these names represent the names of the rulers. If these names are Indian adopted by the Kidarite rulers or the names of later Indian rulers (who might have replaced the Kidarites and the Kidāra coins were slavishly imitated by them), is a matter of further investigation. This type culminated into the coins of the Karkoṭaka dynasty of Kāshmir.

These coins present a fair and firm chronology of the coinage that developed from the coins of Vāsudeva in about third century A.D. and continued up to eighth century A.D. and in a most degenerated form continued still further up to thirteenth or fourteenth century A.D. These coins while presenting a chronology on the basis of the development or degeneration of their fabrics and contents, by themselves, do not provide anything that could help in discerning them into different periods and date their issuers. Only some external evidence may help in this matter.

During my investigations I traced out three hoards of gold coins found in East Punjab (now divided between Pakistan and the Indian States of Punjab and Haryana), which are helpful in dating these coins and their issuers. These hoards were known since long; but little attention was paid to them; they remained untouched for the purpose of history. They contain the coins of one or more varieties of the coins, described above, along with the coins of some Gupta monarchs. The presence of the Gupta coins in these hoards provide a firm date for the internment of the hoards and indicate the time-relation between the Kuṣāṇa rulers and the Gupta monarchs, whose coins are found together in them. They help in cross-check of the chronology of the various types discussed above and fix their place in terms of dates.

One of these hoards was found in 1915 in the village Mithathal in the district of Hisar (now in Haryana Pradesh). It contained 86 gold coins kept in an earthen vessel, which was found while ploughing a field. Of the 86 coins, 26 were melted before the Government machinery could get hold of the find under the Treasure Trove laws. Only 60 coins came in the official hands. Of these 33 coins were related to Samudragupta, (according to the identification of that time; actually 29 of Samudragupta and 4 of Kācagupta) and the remaining 27 were identified as the issues of the Later Kuṣāṇas.[5] The only other information regarding this hoard, that was available for a long time, was that it included a coin of the Battle-axe type of Samudragupta of a rare variety, showing him facing right.[6] While going through the *Annual Reports* of the Central Museum, Lahore, I came to know from the *Report* for the year 1915-16 that the hoard was examined by R.B. Whitehead; and he had prepared a brief Note. According to which, some notable coins in the hoard were : (i) a very fine piece of Samudragupta's Battle-axe type, belonging to a variety of which only one specimen was previously known (the same coin, which finds mention in the Note referred to above); (ii) a coin of Samudragupta of *Aśvamedha* type; and (iii) four coins of Kāca. Whitehead did not say anything about the other coins of Samudragupta and the coins that were called the coins of the Later Kuṣāṇas.

The Museum's *Report* for the year 1916-17, disclosed that 20 coins of the said hoard were acquired by the Museum. The remaining 40 coins, in the possession of the Government might have been distributed to other museums in India and England; but none of the museums has the coins from this hoard. Not unlikely, they might have been either returned to the finder or sold to the public.

Of the 20 coins acquired by the Lahore Museum, 11 belonged to the Guptas and the other 9 were those that were attributed to Later Kuṣāṇas. Of these, 7 coins of Samudragupta and all the 9 coins attributed to the Later Kuṣāṇas are illustrated on two plates in the *Report* without any description or details. The plates, however, help in knowing what coins Lahore Museum had acquired. They show that the coins of Samudragupta acquired by the Museum were:

1. Battle-axe type, king facing right 1
2. *Aśvamedha* type 1
3. Standard type with the name *Samudra* under the left arm 3
4. Standard type with the *Samudragupta* under the left arm 2

With this information in hand, it would not be wrong to assume that the remaining four Gupta coins acquired by the Lahore Museum and not illustrated in the *Report* might be the four coins of Kāca, which Whitehead had mentioned in his *Report* amongst the notables. Further, it would also not be far from the truth to think that the other Gupta coins, that were not acquired by the Lahore Museum, were in all probability, common Standard type coins of Samudragupta. Thus what we have, show that the hoard included the coins of only two Gupta rulers -- Kāca and Samudragupta.

The illustrations of the nine coins, attributed to the Later Kuṣāṇas in the Museum *Report,* disclose that the hoard included the coins of Vāsudeva and post-Vāsudeva rulers as follows:

1. Vāsudeva. *Oeṣo* (Śiva and Bull reverse). No letters in the field. 2
2. Kaniṣka II. *Oeṣo* reverse. Letters *au, ta* and *ga* in the field. 2
3. Kaniṣka III. *Ardokṣo* reverse. Letter *Chu* in the right obverse field. 1
4. Kaniṣka III. *Ardokṣo* reverse. Letters in the obverse field — *Vasu* (on the right), *ga* in the middle and *bha* (on the left). 2
5. Ṣaka. *Ardokṣo* reverse. *Ṣaka* in the right obverse field and *Mi* in the central field. 1

In the light of these coins, it may be presumed that the other coins of this series, that were not acquired, might have been the duplicates of these varieties. It may also be inferred that amongst the twenty coins that did not come to the hands of the Government, if there were any coins of this series, their varieties would have been either the same or similar to them. Now it may be said that the hoard included the coins of Vāsudeva and the Types (ii), (iii) and (iv) of the post-Vāsudeva period, i.e., of Kaniṣka and Ṣaka.

It is well established that the Guptas followed the Kuṣāṇas. And of the two Gupta rulers, represented in this hoard, Kāca, preceded Samudragupta has already been suggested by me on the basis of the analysis of the Gupta coin-hoards[7] and the same is confirmed by this hoard. To suggest the predecessorship of Kāca over Samudragupta, I have pointed out that the coins of Kāca are found mainly in those hoards that include the coins of Candragupta I. Those hoards that do not have the coins of Candragupta I are devoid of the coins of Kāca. Kaserva hoard had the coins only of Kāca and Samudragupta. These two facts taken together place Kāca in between Candragupta I and Samudragupta. The present hoard is very similar to Kaserva hoard, so far as the Gupta coins are concerned. Here the Kuṣāṇa coins are included; they may be said to have taken the place of Candragupta I.

Thus the coins of Samudragupta are the latest in this hoard. Amongst them is a coin of *Aśvamedha* type and the others are only of the Standard and the Battle-axe types. They indicate that the hoard would have been buried not long after the *digvijaya* and the performance of the *Aśvamedha,* i.e., only in the lifetime of Samudragupta. As such it may be said without any fear of contradiction that the hoard was buried some time between A.D. 350 and 370.

The State of Haryana, the area of the find of the hoard, is adjacent to the region of Mathura. The district of Hisar is at a distance of only about 150 kilometers from Mathura. It may well be presumed that the hoard was found in the borderland of the Guptas or the Kuṣāṇas, most likely in the land of the latter. And the typological chronology of the post-Vāsudeva coins, discussed earlier, shows that the coins of the Ṣaka were the latest in the hoard; this amounts to suggest that they were almost contemporary to the coins of Samudragupta; or in other words *Ṣaka* ruler (or rulers) was (were) contemporary to Samudragupta.

These deductions bring to our mind the two phrases *Daivaputra-Ṣāhi-ṣāhānuṣāhi* and *Ṣaka-muruṇḍa* of the Allahabad Pillar Inscription. Most likely these phrases were used for those people, who existed at the border of the Gupta kingdom. With this, I would like to take the liberty to suggest that the term *Ṣaka-muruṇḍa*, used here were none but the *Ṣaka* of the coins. With this, I would like to guess that the circular legend on the coins of *Ṣaka*, written in the cursive Kuṣāṇo-Bactrian script, that appeared like the repetition of 0000, might be the very phrase *Ṣāhi-ṣāhānuṣāhī, Ṣaka-muruṇḍo,* very similar to the legend *Ṣāo Nānoṣāo Kaniṣko Kuṣāṇo. Ṣahī-ṣāhānuṣāhi* is nothing but the transformed *Ṣāo Nānoṣāo* and the personal name *Kaniṣko Kuṣāṇo* was changed with the name of the issuer of the coins as *Ṣaka-muruṇḍo*; and the phrase in the Allahabad *praśasti* was adopted from the coin-legend.

The contents of the hoard, further indiçate that the *Ṣaka* would have displaced the lineage of the Kuṣāṇa Vāsudeva, soon after or in the time of Kaniṣka III. It also shows that Kaniṣka III (Vasu) would not have been at a very long distance from Samudragupta. Keeping in view the possibility of the coins types, included in the hoard, being not exclusive to Kaniṣka III, as is believed by some scholars, there would not have been more than three or four rulers in between Vāsudeva and the *Ṣaka* (or Samudragupta), and their period in no case be more than a century. And if it was so, it amounts to suggest that the Kaniṣka era did not begin in A.D. 78. It would only be somewhere in the mid of the second century A.D.

The second hoard, useful for our purpose, was discovered by Marshall during his excavations at Taxila in a cell, which is designated as *Gc* in Sector *G* of the Dharmarājikā monastery. This hoard contained 19 gold coins; 2 coins belonged to Candragupta II (Archer-type — lotus reverse), 2 were related to Ṣālad with the name *Bhadra* and the remaining 15 coins had the name *Kidāra*.[8] The find of any Gupta coins in the far distant west, away from the boundaries of the empire, is almost unknown. Since Taxila stands on a trade route, it may be suggested that this coin might have filtered there by way of trade; or someone of the Gupta territory might have given them to some monk of the monastery during his wanderings. It could also well have reached there during a military expedition. This brings to our mind the Mehrauli pillar inscription, where it has been said that Candra (Candragupta II) had crossed the seven mouths of (the river) Sindhu (Indus) and reached Vāhlīkas (Bactrians).[9]

The contents of the hoard also show that by this time the post-Vāsudeva rulers of the line of Kaniṣka III had become extinct and the Ṣālada[10] was (or were) then occupying the territory. The Ṣālada might be either contemporary of the Ṣaka or his (or their) successors. In the former case, the inference would be that the Kuṣāṇa territory was divided between two or three small powers Ṣaka, Ṣālada and Gaḍahara (Gaḍakhara), Ṣaka in the east, Ṣālada in the west and Gaḍahara (Gaḍakhara), whose coins are not known in any of the two hoards mentioned here, might have occupied the territory in between the territories of Ṣaka and Ṣālada.[11] There may be another possibility. Ṣālada might have succeeded the Ṣaka over the entire Indian Kuṣāṇa territory. In that case the Ṣālada would have been the contemporary of Candragupta II's expedition to the lands of the seven rivers and beyond the Indus would have weakened the power of this dynasty and given occasion to the Kidārites to penetrate into their region in or about the same time. This is amply clear from the find of 15 coins bearing the name *Kidāra* in the hoard. On the basis of the hoard, the entry of the Kidārites into India may firmly be placed some time round about the end of rule of Candragupta II or beginning of the rule of Kumāragupta I (*circa* 410-420 A.D.). But at that time, they were confined round about the Indus.

The activities of the Kidārites (Kidāras) in India may be inferred, to some extent, on the basis of another hoard, which was found in 1932-33 in the village Machharala in Tahsil Nānkānā Sāheb of the Shekhupura district (Pakistan Punjab). It consisted of only five gold coins and two of them were of the Kidārites. (*Ardokṣo* reverse: *Kidā* under the hand of the king on the obverse); the other three related to the Guptas. Two of them belonged to Skandagupta (Archer type) and the third was the coin of Candragupta II (Archer type—lotus reverse).[12] The presence of the coins of Skandagupta in the hoard indicates that the hoard would have been buried some time during his reign.

The find of the Gupta coins in the hoard in a territory other than their own, situated far off, suggests, a military expedition to that territory. And it also suggests that Skandagupta undertook this military expedition against the Kidārites, when he became king, to repulse the latter's invasion over his kingdom.

Junagarh inscription of Skandagupta speaks that he 'destroyed at its root the pride of his enemies in the *Mleccha* country'.[13] His Bhitari inscription[14] refers to his two conquests with his enemies. In verse 8 of the inscription, his conquest over the Hūṇas is described. Earlier in verse 4, is the mention of a conquest over some enemies (*Yudhyamitrān*); but their name is not specified, nor any other clue is given about them. These enemies, according to the inscription, 'had fully mobilised their resources of manpower and wealth against the Gupta empire and for a time had succeeded in overwhelming its fortune. And Skandagupta was reduced to such a state that he had to spend a whole night in sleeping on bare earth in the battle-field'. Skandagupta ultimately succeeded in inflicting a crushing defeat upon them.

While the Bhitari inscription speaks of the Hūṇas, it is almost certain that he never meant the Kidārites. The Junagarh inscription was recorded within a year or two of his accession. So, it may be presumed that it refers to an engagement with the *Mlecchas*, while he was a prince during the lifetime of his father or just at the very beginning of his reign. Here the inscription may well be interpreted to mean Kidārites, as no other foreign power is known at the threshold of the Indian soil, than the Kidārites, as is evident from the Taxila hoard. The Kidārites, who were in Gandhāra, during the time of Candragupta II, might have made an advance towards the Gupta empire during the time of Kumāragupta I or at the very beginning of Skandaguta's reign. If the Kidārites' movement towards the Gupta empire had taken place during the reign of Kumāragupta I, the present hoard does not mean it. If it took place within first two years of Skandgupta's reign just before the Junagarh inscription was recorded, the presence of his coins along with those of the Kidārites is a possibility.

The enemies, whose crushing defeat is mentioned in the verse 4 of the Bhitari inscription, are considered to be the same as the *Mlecchas* of the Junagarh inscription. It is generally believed that the critical situation, created by the enemies, happened towards the end of Kumāragupta I's reign. But scholars have missed to realise that had this situation occurred at any time before the recording of the Junagarh inscription, the Gupta scribes would not have been satisfied by merely saying what they have said there; they would certainly have been much more eloquent than the scribes of the Bhitari inscription in narrating the chivalrous deeds of Skandagupta as it would have been then fresh in their mind. The absence of any such thing in the Junagarh inscription, means that this event took place only during the later part of the reign of Skandagupta. The verse 6, that says that the conquest was achieved after the death of Kumāragupta I, amounts to suggest only that the enemies that existed from the time of Kumāragupta were crushed by Skandagupta after the former's death. And these enemies (*yudhyamitrān*) would naturally have been the same, who were defeated earlier and called *Mlecchas* in the Junagarh inscription. It was natural for them that having been defeated once at the hands of Skandagupta, to mobilise their manpower and wealth fully against the Gupta empire to avenge their humiliating defeat; and it was equally natural for Skandagutpa to call them by the name of *yudhyamitrān*.

It appears that the Machharala hoard is connected with this event; the Kidārites, after being defeated by Skandagupta, retreated back towards the Punjab; and Skandagupta's army marched long way to push them back as far as possible. To conclude, the Machharala hoard indicates that the Gupta rulers were not indifferent towards the Punjab, as has been considered so far.

References

1. *The Vākāṭaka-Gupta Age,* p. 28, 37-38.
2. *J.U.P.H.S.,* XXII, 1950, p. 172.
3. *C.I.I.,* III, pp. 1ff; line 23.
4. *Later Indo-Scythians,* 1962, p. 28.
5. *A.S.I., A.R.,* 1915-16, p. 19.
6. *Ibid.,* 1926-27, p. 233-34; It is also mentioned by Altekar, *The Coinage of the Gupta Empire,* p. 309.
7. *The Imperial Guptas,* Varanasi; 1974, p. 96.
8. Marshall, *Taxila,* p. 283, 822.
9. *C.I.I.,* III, p. 139; *S.I.,* p. 2275, line 2; Lately an archaeological exploration expedition conducted by A.H. Dani discovered a number of small inscriptions bearing the names of Candragupta and Hariṣeṇa on the boulders on the ancient Karkoram road. They indicate that Candragupta's army passed that way.
10. This is one of the readings of the name and is that Marshall had adopted in his *Taxila* in the follow of V. Smith. Later R.D. Banerji has emended it as Ṣīlada. Earlier it was read by F.W. Thomas as ṣaṇḍi. Cunningham had read it variously: Pakindha, Paskindha, Pahalandhi. In recent years it has been read as Nipunadha (Joe Cribb), Kipanada (Mitchiner), Kṣiṇaṭha and Skiṇaṭha (Mitterwallner). I now feel Thomas was more correct in his reading.
11. Incidentally, it may be pointed out that the coins related to Gaḍakhara (Gaḍahara) that bear the name *Samudra,* are considered by scholars, to refer to the Gupta emperor Samudragupta and they suggest that it indicates the sovereignty of the latter, the Gaḍahara (Gaḍakhara) and the allied tribes. But the suggestion, on its very face is in no acceptable. If *Samudra* meant on the coins the Gupta emperor, then *Kīrada* and the other names appearing on the coins of Gaḍahara at the same place should also mean the names of the sovereigns of the Gaḍahara people. But no such power is known with these other names. Corrollary to the suggestion, would be that Sita, Bhadra and other names seen on the coins of Ṣaka and Ṣālada were also the names of the sovereign rulers; but in their case, the names are considered to be those of the subordinates or governors, under these people and not their sovereigns. Apart from these inconsistencies, the invalidity of these views is clear from the Taxila hoard. It clearly shows that Gaḍahara could not be the contemporary of Samudragupta; if they were contemporary to any Gupta emperor, they would have been only of Candragupta II.
12. Lahore Museum Report for the year 1932-33.
13. *C.I.I.,* III, p. 57, line 3.
14. *Ibid.,* p. 52ff. Verses 4 and 8.

9

Quarter-Stater of Kaniṣka*

I

THE photographs reproduced here *(fig. 18)* were given to me by a friend, who got it from one of his friends in Vārāṇasī. These photographs were brought to the Vārāṇasī friend by a dealer of eastern Uttar Pradesh and on the basis of these photographs, he wanted to sell the coin which, he said, was in the possession of another person. He said that he would bring the coin when the 'price is agreed on the basis of the photographs'. On being insisted upon showing the coin before anything was committed for the purchase of the coin, the dealer promised to bring the coin. But he never turned up. He however, informed that the coin was sold. Thus the whereabouts of the coin are not known.

Since the coin appears interesting and rare, I publish it here on the basis of the photographs.

The weight and size of the coin are not known; but the smaller photograph, given here (*fig. 18a-b*), represents the actual size of the coin. By the size, the coin appears to be a quarter-stater, which would have weighed in the proximity of 2 grammes. The coin may be described as follows:

> ***Obv.:*** Head of the king in profile to left emerges from rock or clouds; wearing low cap, projecting the lower end outward at front and back, a circular spot over the

---

* Originally published in *Numismatic Digest*, V.ii (1981), pp. 23-24. Author: Sarojini Kulashreshtha.

cap. Behind the head something like the fluttering end of a turban. The king wears long bushy beard with the lower end widely spread and the hair clearly delineated. Legend around, most likely beginning from I but very much truncated and blurred; only two *K*s may be seen, one near about *V* and other close to VIII.

Rev.: Four-armed Śiva wearing *dhotī and yajñopavīta,* standing frontally to left, holding objects in upper and lower right hands, not clear; in the upper upraised left hand a long trident: the lower left hand placed on hip holding by horns a *mṛga* (an antelope or stag). Symbol on the lower left and legend OEṢO (to be read inside) on the right. (*fig. 18,* original and enlarged)

The fabric, execution and devices leave no doubt that the coin belongs to a Kuṣāṇa king, but due to the truncated blurred obverse legend, its attribution to any king is problematic. The two *K*s of the legend suggest that one may stand for Kaniṣka and the other for Kuṣāṇa. The legend might have been *Ṣāo Nāno Ṣāo Kaneṣki(o) Koṣāṇo.*

The bust-type Kuṣāṇa coins are known to have been issued only by two rulers Vima Kadphises and Huviṣka. Bust-type coins of Kaniṣka are not known. But a coin of bust-type exists in the British Museum: and curiously enough it is also, like this coin, a quarter-stater. So, if the conjecture about the obverse legend is correct, there is no difficulty in attributing this coin to Kaniṣka.

The difficulty, however, lies in the fact that the portrait-head does not resemble any head depicted on the coins of Kaniṣka. On all the coins of Kaniṣka the lower end of the king's beard is shown rounded; and it is not very long. Here the beard is not only very long but also straight trimmed in a line at the bottom. Thus we cannot be sure that the head actually represents Kaniṣka.

Presuming that the coin belongs to Kaniṣka. It does not conform in any way to the devices seen on the quarter-stater of Kaniṣka in the British Museum. Not only the portrait is distinctly different, the reverse divinity is also different. On the British Museum coin he is Athśo, whereas here he is Oeṣo (Śiva). The only thing common on the two coins is the reverse symbol.

If, this coin is of Kaniṣka, it is so far the only one of its kind. It is a pity that we do not know about its existence.

II*

The quarter-stater of Kaniṣka, described in the above Note[1], is republished by T.P. Verma[2] with some comments upon my Note.

In his Note, Verma has misrepresented my views by saying that I doubt the genuineness of the coin, while in my Note there was not one word which could give the slightest impression of any such doubt. I have only pointed out the dissimilarities that I perceived in the portrait depicted on this coin from those that are usually seen on the well-known staters of Kaniṣka (I). One may at best infer from my words that I do not think that this is a coin of Kaniṣka (I), but never that it was forged or fake. There have been occasions in Indian numismatics when scholars have differed widely in the attribution or identification of coins; but never has a scholar accused another, whose opinion differed from his, doubting the nature of the coin.

I would not have argued with Verma had it been the simple matter of perceiving the portraiture on the coin. I would have readily accepted that his vision might be better than mine. But something else prompted me when I made my observations. And that was the legend on the coin. The legend on the coin is very much truncated. So, I merely expressed the probability of its beginning at 1 o'clock and refrained from drawing further conclusions out of it. But Verma has now made it easy for me to open my mind by his own admission that the legend on the

---

* Originally published in *Numismatic Digest*, IX (1985), pp. 46-51. Author: Sarojini Kulashreshtha.

coin begins at 12 o'clock which is very close to my presumption. He has no doubts about his statement as he has fixed the place of each and every letter of the legend around the illustration of the coin that he has appended to his Note.

Verma, being a University teacher of Numismatics and Editor of the Journal of an august Society of Numismatics, would be better equipped than me to know that the legends on the obverse of the coins of the Kuṣāṇa rulers, Kaniṣka, Huviṣka and Vāsudeva always began, without exception, at about VII o'clock, and that on those Kuṣāṇa coins that were issued during the post-Vāsudeva period bear, without exception, legends that began only about XII or I o'clock. In the light of these facts, it is admitted by scholars that any Kuṣāṇa coin with the obverse legend beginning at XII or I o'clock, would not belong to any period earlier than that of Vāsudeva. The legend on the quarter-stater in question begins a XII or I o'clock; so, in no case, it can be attributed to Kaniṣka I. If the coin does not belong to Kaniṣka I, it is immaterial whether the portrait on the coin has any similarity or dissimilarity from the portraits on the staters of Kaniṣka I. Was I wrong if I did not preceive on the coin those similarities to the portrait of Kaniṣka I which Verma has tried to see ?

Verma has also tried to impress upon the readers that I have made certain contentions about the Kuṣāṇa coinage. I am not in a position to make any kind of contentions. I am in no way a scholar of numismatics like him; my access to literature on Kuṣāṇa numismatics also is very much limited. I can but repeat what I have read; and I have narrated only what is generally known to numismatists about the bust-type Kuṣāṇa coins, that 'they are known to have been issued only by two rulers Vima-Kadphises and Huviṣka'. To this statement I have added 'Bust-type coins of Kaniṣka are not known'. My statement thus is crystal clear and there is no chance of any ambiguity or misunderstanding. Yet Verma has tried to put me in the wrong by deliberately quoting me partially.

Verma has then raised a point about the contents of the

cabinet of the British Museum. I would confess, here too, that I do not have that much access to the British Museum cabinet as Verma might have. So, I would rather go by his own words. He informs us 'Quarter-staters were issued by Vima, Kaniṣka, Huviṣka and Vāsudeva. Five varieties of this denomination are known in the British Museum: 2 Athśo type, 1 Nānā Ṣāo type, 1 Ordoxo type and 2 Oeṣo type.' He adds that of the two Oeṣo type coins, on one the bust is depicted'.[3] He has, however, not mentioned who the kings represented by these types are, i.e., has not specifically explained. How one is to know that he was speaking about any quarter-stater of Kaniṣka? What he has said about the bust-type quarter-stater would apparently lead to the presumption that the coin would be relating to Huviṣka or Vima, whose bust-type coins are well-known. Elsewhere[4] he states, 'As we have discussed earlier, there are three quarter-staters of Kaniṣka and two of these bear king's bust on the obverse'. But no where I could find his 'earlier discussion', where he might have mentioned specifically the bust-type quarter-staters of Kaniṣka. I might be unaware of the exact contents of the coins in the British Museum; but nowhere my statement is confusing as is this one of Verma. Further clarity is needed in his statements to understand him better.

The readers, at any rate, would be thankful to him for correcting me and informing them that the British Museum possesses not one but two bust-type quarter-staters of Kaniṣka — one each of Athśo and Oeṣo types. But at the same time I would still like to point out to him that he might not be correct in his belief that the present coin was the fourth quarter-stater of Kaniṣka (I). I cannot be sure that the full figure-type coin of this denomination in the British Museum would be only one. British Museum has acquired many more such coins since the *Catalogue* was published on which he has relied for his statement. The full-figure quarter-staters of Kaniṣka are not so rare as Verma presumes. There are at least three such specimen in the Bhārat Kalā Bhavan, which is located in the very campus of the Benaras Hindu University, where he teaches Numismatics. They represent Miiro, Pharro and Nānā Ṣāo on their reverse.

The bust-type quarter-staters also are not confined to two specimens in the British Museum. Verma might not be aware that a quarter-stater of the Athśo type exists in the State Museum, Lucknow also; there it has been lying for more than half a century. The present coin, as such, is not the third but the fourth of its kind. If all these coins can be attributed to Kaniṣka (I) in the light of what I have pointed out above is very much doubtful.

Lastly, it is not of much consequence to know the whereabouts of the present coin. But Verma has made an issue to put me in the dock and say that I am not only misinformed but confused. He might be correct in saying that the coin exists with Ram Rup Gupta of Jaunpur. But I cannot be sure of it. Verma might be fortunate enough to see the coin; but the fact remains that to whom-so-ever Ram Rup Gupta offered the coin for sale, he never showed the coin. He always tried to trade on the basis of the photographs. I can confidently assert that not only the private collectors were not allowed to see the coins, but the museums, to which he offered it for sale, were also not given any chance to see the coin. This might be one reason why the coin remained unsold.[5] Whatever I said in my last Note and again I repeat it, is not a story, as Verma presumes; but is the account of a respectable coin-collector who had given me the photographs that I have published. No one, who knows him personally, would disbelieve him. He might be misinformed; in that case, the misinformant was none else but Gupta himself. Verma should now realise who in fact is confused.

Addenda

Since writing this Note I came to know that the Bust-type quarter-staters of Kaniṣka are not so rare as Verma and myself had presumed. They are well-known today as are his quarter-staters of the Standing-type. The only thing is that Indian scholars are not much aware of them. They do not have any easy access to the literature published outside India. The latest work on the Kuṣāṇa numismaitcs is R. Göbl's Atlas of the Kuṣāṇa coins in German language. It records 17 coin of Kaniska of the Bust and 18 of the Standing types. The Bust-type coins, known to Göbl are:[6]

1. ATHŚO.	1. Source not disclosed.
	2-3. British Museum (Unpublished)
	4. British Museum (*B.M.C.* 26.11; Rosenfield 35).
	5. Published by Zeymal (Probably in the Hermitage Museum, Leningrad).
	6-7. Collection of G.A. Gai, Peshawar.
	8. American Numismatic Society, New York.
	9. Lahore Museum (*P.M.C.*, 17.67)
	10. Collection of C.A. Burns, California, U.S.A.
2. MAO.	11. British Museum (Rosenfield 101).
3. NANA.	12. British Museum (Rosenfield 160).
	13. British Museum (Unpublished)
	14. American Numismatic Society, New York.
	15. Collection of C.A. Burns, California.
4. OEṢO.	16. British Museum (*B.M.C.*, 26.16)
	17. British Museum (Unpublished).

This inventory shows that the British Museum possesses eight coins; of which only two are recorded in the Museum's *Catalogue*. Another coin from the Museum is illustrated by Rosenfield (Mao, 101). Five coins are unpublished, of which none of the scholars in India could know. They, however, could well know about the three published ones. Verma consulted *B.M.C.* and missed Rosenfield; I had consulted Rosenfield; but then I could notice only coin (no. 36) and not the other two (nos. 101, 160). Punjab Museum has a coin; but none of these scholars realised its existence. To Göbl's inventory, we may add two more coins; one that is published above; the other is in the State Museum, Lucknow, which is unpublished and is pointed out by me above. A third coin having ATHŚO on the reverse would be a further addition, if it is not anyone out of Nos. 1 and 10 of the above list. It has just come to notice in an auction catalogue of an American numismatic dealer. It was to be auctioned on December 10, 1980. The coins of this type can in no circumstances be termed rare.

However, the rarity of the coins is not so important as their attribution. Göbl has illustrated six coins out of the seventeen and all of them, like the coin under discussion, have the obverse circular legend as beginning at XII or I o'clock. I have rightly pointed out that the legend on the coins of Kaniṣka and his successors Huviṣka and Vāsudeva begins at about VII o'clock. As such, I am perfectly justified in questioning the attribution of the bust-type quarter-staters to Kaniṣka I. I have also pointed out that the legends beginning at XII or I o'clcok are found only on the post-Vāsudeva coins. This virtually means that the coin belonged to a ruler named Kaniṣka of the post-Vāsudeva period, though I have not specifically said so in the above Note.

In the post-Vāsudeva period existed two rulers named Kaniṣka - II and III. Which of these two Kaniṣkas had issued these quarter-staters, is not easy to say. But in view of the fact that Stater-coins of Kaniṣka II have Oeṣo while these of Kaniṣka III have Ardokṣo on their reverse, it is quite likely that these quarter-staters were issued by Kaniṣka II. Amongst his stater-coins, Oeṣo type is well known and the Ardokṣo type is conspecious there by its absence. Stylisticly, these coins are close to the coins of Vāsudeva.

References

1. *N.D.,* V, Part II, pp. 23-24.
2. A Quarter Stater of Kaniṣka, *J.N.S.I.,* XLV, 1983, pp. 36-39.
3. *Ibid.,* p. 37.
4. *Ibid.,* p. 38.
5. The coin is now in the State Museum, Lucknow. Purchased after the paper was published.
6. *Munzaprägung des Kušānreiches,* Wein, 1984, p. 102, Nos. 41-45, Pl. 6.

10

Coins of Vaśiṣka*

While looking through the illustrations of the Kuṣāṇa coins given by Rosenfield in his *Dynastic Arts of the Kuṣāṇas,* I noticed that one of the coins from the British Museum described by him as the coin of Kaniṣka III[1] bears a legend different from that found on the coins of this ruler. The coin is illustrated here *(fig. 19).*

The legend on this coin, between I and V o'clock, is truncated; but the traces of the letters are clear enough to show that it was ṢAO NANO ṢAO. Then between VII and XI o'clock the letters are clear and they may easily be read as BAZEṢKO KOṢAN[O]. B.N. Mukherjee has also noticed this very legend — BAZEṢKO KOṢANO on another coin[2] which also was originally identified as the coin of Kaniṣka III.[3] This coin was found in a hoard of 33 Kuṣāṇa gold coins discovered in the village Dalhupur in Jaunpur district (Uttar Pradesh).[4] The coin is illustrated here (*fig. 20*).

Neither to Mukherjee nor to me belongs the claim of having discovered the coins of Bazeṣko (Vaśiṣka). Much before we noticed these coins, Göbl had already discovered the name BAZEṢKO on some other coins. He found this name first in 1966 on four coins — two in the British Museum, London, one in the Ashmoleon Museum, Oxford, and one in the Peshawar Museum.[5] Later, he included these coins in his book on the Iranian Hūṇas of Bactria and India.[6] In 1979, he published three more coins of

* Originally published in *Numismatic Digest,* X (1988), pp. 70-80. Author: Sarojini Kulashreshtha.

Vaśiṣka — the first from some private collection, the second from the British Museum and the third from the American Numismatic Society.[7] On all these coins published by Göbl the name of the ruler is either truncated or partially available; and the coin, mentioned above, does not figure amongst the British Museum coins illustrated by him. As such, this coin is an addition to the list of Vaśiṣka's coins.[8]

All these coins invariably bear on the obverse a trident in the field behind the alter, which is the peculiarity of the later (post-Vāsudeva) coinage. The Ardokṣo reverse of these coins closely links them with the coins of Kaniṣka III. So it may well be said that Vaśiṣka, the issuer of these coins, was a ruler of post-Vāsudeva period, close to Kaniṣka III.

A king named Vaśiṣka is known from the following inscriptions :

1. Two inscribed Buddhist sculptures of Mathura origin found at Sanchi, record the reigning kings as *Rājña Vaskuṣāṇa*[9] and *Mahārājasya rajatirājasya devaputrasya Ṣāhi-Vaśiṣka.*[10] They are dated in the years 22 and 28 respectively and show that a king named Vaśiṣka (Vasi[ṣka][11] Kuṣāṇa) existed in these years.

2. A *yūpa*-pillar, discovered at Īsāpur (near Mathura) bears the inscription *Mahārājasya rajtirājasya devaputrasya Ṣāher Vaśiṣkasya rājya-samvatsarye Caturvviṁśe.*[12] This inscription means that a king named Vaśiṣka was reigning in the year 24.

3. A Kharoṣṭhī inscription, found at Ārā near Attack in Pakistan, bears the following words: *Maharajasa rajatirajasa devaputrasa Kāisarasa Vajheṣkaputrasa Kaniṣkasa saṁvatsarae Cahaparisae* 20 20 1 (i.e., 41).[13] This shows that there was a Kaniṣka who was reigning in the year 41 and was the son of Vajheṣka (Vaśiṣka).

Vaśiṣka of all these inscriptions had been placed so far by most scholars amongst the early Kuṣāṇa rulers. So in contradistinction to Vaśiṣka of the inscriptions, Vaśiṣka of the coins is designated by Göbl and Mukherjee as Vaśiṣka II, which means that Vaśiṣka of the inscriptions was Vaśiṣka I.

Believing that the dates in all these inscriptions were reckoned in the Kaniṣka (Kuṣāṇa) era, it is pointed out by scholars that the years 22 to 41 overlap the reigns of the Kuṣāṇa rulers Kaniṣka and Huviṣka. This apparent anachronism is explained by the hypothesis of their co-rulership. According to them, Vaśiṣka was a co-ruler with Kaniṣka I during the years 22 and 23 and thereafter with Huviṣka. Again in the same vein, Kaniṣka of the Ārā inscription is identified as Kaniṣka II; he also is suggested to be co-ruler with Huviṣka in the year 41.

I propose to point out in this context, that Vaśiṣka named in the inscriptions and the coin-legends was one and the same and not two different rulers existing in two different periods.

Many stone sculptures, carved at Mathura bear inscriptions with dates ranging from year 2 to 98, which are adjudged by scholars as the era of Kaniṣka (Kuṣāṇa). While reconstructing the relative chronology of the Mathura school of art, Lohuizen has pointed out that some of these sculptures bear such elements that are of much later period than the dates mentioned on them. She has isolated such sculptures and suggested that they were the products of post-Vāsudeva period and the figure 100 was omitted on them,[14] i.e., they were 100 years later in date than those inscribed on them. If these dates are to be reckoned in the continuation of Kaniṣka (Kuṣāṇa) era, 100 should be added to them. It would be more simple to say that these Mathura sculptures were dated in an era that was different from the Kaniṣka (Kuṣāṇa) era. This new era began afresh a century later with the year 1. It may be called second Kuṣāṇa era.

Lohuizen placed one of the two Sanchi sculptures, referred to above, in the post-Vāsudeva period on the basis of stylistic properties that she had discerned in the later Kuṣāṇa sculptures. She considered Vaskuṣāṇa of its inscription as one of Vāsudeva's successors.[15] The second sculpture was mutilated; so she did not say anything about it. But Rosenfield has discussed both the Sanchi sculptures and, according to him, both of them relate to a much later period than that of Kaniṣka and Huviṣka.[16] He has tentatively suggested that the king mentioned in the inscriptions of these sculptures may be reflected in the series of coins that have the name Vasu.[17] In simple terms, he means to say that these sculptures are post-Vāsudeva.

If the conclusions drawn by Lohuizen and Rosenfield about the period of these scultpures and the discovery of the coins bearing the name Vaśiṣka are taken together, they leave no room to speculate about the identity of Vaśiṣka mentioned in the inscriptions. One of the two sculptures clearly mentions the name Vaśiṣka. There can be no hesistation in identifying him with Vaśiṣka of the coins. The date of this inscription is so close to that of the second Sanchi sculpture that it would also not be ureasonable to postulate that the sculpture on which it is engraved belonged to the period of Vaśiṣka of the coins. The date of the Īsāpur *yūpa*-inscription, mentioning Vaśiṣka, falls in between the two dates of Sanchi inscriptions. Like them, this inscription may easily be attributed to Vaśiṣka of the coins.

In addition to relying on the conclusions drawn by Lohuizen and Rosenfield to place the Sanchi and Īsāpur inscriptions in the post-Vāsudeva period and to identify their Vaśiṣka with Vaśiṣka of the coins, we have an independent evidence in the contents of these inscriptions. It shows that they could not be assigned to any date earlier than the post-Vāsudeva period; and this evidence is quite conclusive.

This evidence is implicit in the fact that all the inscriptions of Kaniṣka, Huviṣka and Vāsudeva (before the year 84) employ for them the titles *Mahārāja rajatirāja Devaputra,*[18] while the Sanchi and Īsāpur inscriptions bear the titles *Mahārāja rajatirāja Devaputra Ṣāhi* for Vaśiṣka. Here is an additional title *Ṣāhi* which, coupled with the usual titles *Mahārāja rajatirāja Devaputra,* is seen for the first time in the inscriptions of Vāsudeva dated after the year 83;[19] and thereafter in a number of inscriptions on the sculptures placed by Lohuizen in the post-Vāsudeva period.[20] This evidently means that the additional title *Ṣāhi* was introduced only in the later part of the reign of Vāsudeva. If this additional title is found in the Sanchi and Īsāpur inscriptions, the only conclusion would be that they were not in any case earlier than the period of Vāsudeva; and the king Vaśiṣka, mentioned in them, was none other than the issuer of the gold coins.

However, there are two Mathura inscriptions that have the epithet *Ṣāhi* used for persons deemed to be Great Kuṣāṇa, i.e., pre-Vāsudeva rulers. They may be cited against the aforesaid conclusions. They need to be thoroughly examined.

One of them is inscribed on an enthroned image found at Māṭ near Mathura[21] and reads as *Mahārāja rajatirāja Devaputra Kuṣāṇaputra Ṣāhi Vematakṣama.* Here *Vematakṣama* is identified by scholars as Vima Kadphises. If it was so, this inscription would go against the above conclusions. But the identification of *Vematakṣama* with Vima Kadphises is based merely on the fact that *Vema* is common in both the names. The second part of the names, which is crucial, is ignored. Vima Kadphises is known in the inscriptions either as *Vima* or *Vimakaphsa.* If the inscription meant to convey that it was the effigy of Vima Kadphises, it would have used the familiar forms of his name rather than this obscure *Takṣama.* The word *Takṣama* can in no way be equated with Kadphises (*Kaphasa*), either philologically or phonetically. Moreover, the titles *Mahārāja rajatirāja Devaputra Kuṣāṇaputra Ṣāhi* used in this inscription need careful scrutiny. Most notable here is the title *Kuṣāṇaputra.* The Kuṣāṇa rulers were always called *Kuṣāṇa* and never *Kuṣāṇaputra* either in inscriptions or on coins. This is most significant and shows that Vematakṣama was only a collateral and not a direct descendent of the Kuṣāṇas. Therefore, he should not be confused with Vima Kadphises. The title *Ṣāhi* would place him only amongst the rulers of the later period and never amongst the Great Kuṣāṇas.

The second inscription is known as Puṇyaśālā inscription. It is dated in the year 28 of an unspecified era, though generally believed to be the Kaniṣka (Kuṣāna) era. It was first published by K.P. Jayaswal[22] then it was edited by Sten Konow;[23] Lastly, it is mentioned by D.C. Sircar.[24] In the case of this inscription, it has not been realised that the name of the reigning king, which was invariably mentioned in the Kuṣāṇa inscriptions found at Mathura along with the date, conspicuously absent. This is quite significant. We cannot be sure as to who was the reigning king when the inscription was recorded. Still more significant is the fact that the merits (*puṇya*) of the pious deeds are bestowed upon the person, who is named in lines 9-10. If he was the reigning king Huviṣka, it is extremely surprising that his regal titles *Mahārāja* or *Mahārāja rajatirāja*, used in all the Mathura inscriptions of the Kuṣāṇas without exception, for the rulers, are ignored. The donor of the endowment was himself a state officer — officer-in-charge of religious establishments (*bakanapati*). It can never be imagined that any state-officer would ever be so imprudent as to defy all the royal decorum and refer to his master, the reigning king, simply with an auxiliary title *Ṣāhi*, more so, when he was sacrificing his *puṇya* in his favour. These two facts are enough to convince that the person, mentioned in lines 9-10, could not be the reigning king, even if his name was Huviṣka.

This inscription is incised on one side of the bottom rectangular part of a pillar, which is now located in the Mathura Museum, which is only at a stone's throw from my place. So, I could easily see and examine it myself.[25] It would be a great surprise to scholars to know that nowhere in the inscription is the name of *Huviṣka*. What is there is line 10 is *Puviṣka* which cannot be read by any stretch of imagination as *Huviṣka*. Though Konow has accepted the name Huviṣka in the text of the inscription, he was quite conscious of this fact. He has honestly admitted, in a footnote to his paper that it looks like *Puviṣka*. It is only Sircar, who, without providing any information about the actual engraving, has accepted *Huviṣka* in the text. Konow and Sircar knew no person other than the reigning monarch with the name ending in *viṣka* so it seems that they were prompted to assume that it meant only Huviṣka. But this was hardly any reason for any scholar to emend the historical document in this manner.

As eminent epigraphists and palaeographists, both the scholars might have well observed that there was hardly any paleographical fault in this inscription. They might also have been aware that even those engravers, who have committed serious palaeographical faults in their engravings, did never falter with the name of the reigning monarchs. They did some time shorten the names, knowingly or unknowingly;[26] but in no instance did they misconstrue the initial parts of the name. Yet, they believed that the engraver had faulted here in the king's name. Any way, by their emendation of the actual name engraved on the stone, they have created a wrong belief amongst the scholars about this inscription. It should now be corrected.

The actual name being Puviṣka or Praviṣka in the inscription, there is no reason to say that it belongs to the period of Huviṣka. It should now, in the light of my observations that the title *Ṣāhi* was used only in the post-Vāsudeva period, be taken as a post-Vāsudeva inscription and concluded that the date mentioned therein was in the second Kuṣāṇa era. This would perhaps find support from its script. I am no palaeograhist; yet to me it appears that it is more akin to the script of early Gupta inscriptions than to that of the early Kuṣāṇa inscriptions.

Thus the path is well paved to identify Vaśiṣka of the coins with Vaśiṣka of Sanchi and Īsāpur Inscriptions. It may now be said conveniently and convincingly that there was only one Vaśiṣka and he flourished in the post-Vāsudeva period.

We are now left with the Ārā Inscription, which is dated in the year 41 and refers to *Mahārājā rajatirāja Kaisara Vajheṣkaputra Kaniṣka*. Here is a title *kaisara,* which is unknown elsewhere in the Kuṣāṇa inscriptions. It is generally recognised that this title for the Kuṣāṇa king is influenced by the title of the Roman emperors, but it is perhaps not realised that it meant almost the same as the title *Ṣāhi*. To me it appears that the title *kaisara* is possibly used here as the synonym of *Ṣāhi*. If this presumption is accepted, there should be no difficulty in placing this inscription in the line of Sanchi and Īsāpur Inscriptions. Even otherwise there is no difficulty in placing it with them.

In the present context what needs to be noticed is, that in this inscription mentions the name of Kaniṣka as the son of Vaśiṣka (Vajheṣka). The coins of Vaśiṣka are so close and similar in their fabric, style and contents to the coins of Kaniṣka III that scholars have missed the distinction between them. The two might be successive issues of father and son. Accordingly, Vaśiṣka and Kaniṣka, father and son of the Ārā inscription, may be identified with Vaśiṣka and Kaniṣka III of the coins.

The discovery of the coins of Vaśiṣka, thus eliminates the existence of the hypothetical Vaśiṣka and Kaniṣka II from the history of the Great Kuṣāṇas and places them in the realm of reality, amongst the rulers of the post-Vāsudeva period. It may now conveniently be said that the king named Vaśiṣka existed in the post-Vāsudeva period between the years [1]22 and [1]28; and that his son was Kaniṣka III (known from the Ārā Inscription and supported by coins); he ruled in the year [1]41. This Kaniṣka may be placed earlier in the year [1]30 or [1]40 if the fragmentary inscription on the pedestal of a seated Buddha image from Mathura, now in Indian Museum, Calcutta[27] could be restored as *Mahārājasya Deva[putrasya] [Ka]niṣkasya saṁ 30 (or 40) he [4] di [10 4].*[28]

Kaniṣka II, though ousted from the earlier period of Kuṣāṇa history, is not eliminated. He would now be Kaniṣka, not of Ārā Inscription but of those Mathura sculptures that have the artistic properties of the post-Vāsudeva period and bear the name Kaniṣka with the dates7,[29] 9,[30] 14[31] and 17[32]. Two of the inscriptions[33] of these sculptures also bear the additional title *Ṣāhi* for the king. His coins may well be isolated from amongst the existing coins that were so far being attributed to Kaniṣka III. To me those coins of post-Vāsudeva Kaniṣka that have *Oeṣo* on the reverse are the coins of this king and only those that have Ardokṣo on the reverse belong to Kaniṣka III.[34]

References

1. Rosenfield, *Dynastic Arts,* Pl. XII, coin 240; p. 109.

2. B.N. Mukherjee, "A Gold Coin of Bazeṣko", *J.N.S.I.,* XXXIV, 1972, p. 31.

3. A.K. Srivastava, A hoard of Kuṣāṇa Coins from Jaunpur district, *B.M.A.,U.P.* No. 4 (December 1969), p. 29, fig. 12.

4. *Ibid.*, pp. 27-30.
5. R. Göbl, Vaśiṣka II, ein bisher unbekannter konig de spatare Kuṣāṇ, *Osterreichische Akademie der Wissenschaftern Kommissionverlag*, Jahrganj 1965, No. 11, pp. 285-300.
6. R. Göbi, *Dokumente zur Geschichte der Iranischen Hunnen in Baktrien und Inden*, Wissbaden, 1967, Vol. II, pp. 312-13; Vol. IV, Pl. I, 16; pl. VIII, 1-4.
7. R. Göbl, Vaśiṣka, Vāskuṣāṇa and Xodasah, *Verlag der Osterreichischen Akademie der Wissenschaften*, 1979, 111, So. 11, pp. 118-25.
8. Since this paper was originally written, R. Göbl has published a monumental atlas of Kuṣāṇa coins includes many more coins of Vaśiṣka *Munzpragung des Kusanreiches*, Wein, 1984, pl. 35.
9. Marshall and Foucher, *Sanchi*, Pl. 105c: p. 386.
10. *Ibid*, Pl. 124b; p. 285; G. Bühler, "Further Votive Inscriptions at Sanchi", *E.I.*, II, p. 269ff; H. Luders, Three Early Brāhmī Inscriptions, *ibid*, IX, p. 244.
11. The engraver has perhaps missed the letters *śka* and incised Vaśiṣka Kuṣāṇa as *Vaṣkusāṇa* in the inscription dated 22. Such omission is noticed also in a Mathura inscription where Huviska is engraved as *Huṣka* (Kānakli Tilā Jain Image in Lucknow Museum), G. Bühler, "Further Jain Inscriptions from Mathura", *ibid*, II, p. 206.
12. J. Ph. Vogel, "The Sacrificial Post of Īsāpur", *A.S.I., AR*, 1910-11, pp. 40-48.
13. Sten Konow, "Ārā (Kharoṣṭhī) Inscription of Kaniṣka II", *E.I.*, XIV, pp. 130-43.
14. Lohuizen, *The Scythian Period in Indian History*, Leiden, 1949, pp. 237 ff.
15. *Ibid.*, pp. 312-14.
16. Rosenfield, *op. cit.*, p. 295, note 22.
17. *Ibid*, p. 113.
18. Kaniṣka — *Mahārāja rajatirāja Devaputra* (Mat portrait, Mathura Museum) J.P. Vogel, Explorations at Mathura, *A.S.I.,A.R.*, 1911-12, pp. 122 ff.

    10 *Mahārāja Devaputra* (Dedicatory Inscription, British Museum), H. Luders, "Three Early Brahmi Inscriptions", *I.A.*, IX, pp. 239-41.

    Huviṣka 33 *Mahārāja Devaputra* (Buddhist Image, Lucknow Museum), T. Bloch, "Two Inscriptions on Buddhist Images", *E.I.*, VIII, p. 181.

		35	*Mahārāja Devaputra* (Lucknow Bodhisattva, Mathura Museum), Rosenfield, *op. cit.*, p. 267.
		40	*Mahārāja Rajatirāja* (Chargaon Nagaraja, Mathura Museum), Rosenfield *op. cit.*, p. 267.
		45	*Mahārāja Devaputra* (Buddhist Image, Bombay University), Rosenfield, *op. cit.*, p. 267.
		50	*Mahārāja Devaputra* (Buddhist Image, Mathura Museum), Rosenfield, op. cit., p. 267.
		53.	*Mahārāja Devaputra,* (Naroli Buddhist Image Pedestal, Mathura Museum), Rosenfield, *op. cit.*, p. 167).
		60	*Mahārāja rajatirāja Devaputra* (Kankali Tilā Jain Image, Lucknow *E.I.*, Museum), G. Bühler, "New Jain Inscriptions from Mathura", *E.I.*, p. 286).
	Vāsudeva	78	*Mahārāja rajatirāja Devaputra* (Jamalpur Stone Slab, Indian Museum), G. Bühler, New Jain Inscriptions from Mathura, *ibid.* I, p. 373).
19.	Vāsudeva	84	*Mahārāja rajatirāja Devaputra Ṣāhi* (Balbhadrakunda Jain Image, Mathura Museum), Rosenfield, *op. cit.*, p. 269.
		87.	*Mahārāja rajatirāja Ṣāhi* (Kankali Tilā Jain Image, Mathura Museum), *C.A.S.R.* III. p. 35.
20.	Kaniṣka II	17	*Mahārāja rajatirāja Devaputra Ṣāhi* (Kānkali Tilā Jain Image, Lucknow Museum), G. Bühler, "New Jain Inscriptions from Mathura", *E.I.* p. 391.
		17	*Devaputra Ṣāhi* (Kānkali Tilā Jain Image, Rosenfield, *op. cit.*, p. 271).

21. J. Ph. Vogel, "Explorations at Mathuā", *A.S.I.A.R.* 1911-12, p. 120.

22. *J.B.O.R.S.*, XVIII, pp. 4ff, plate facing p. 6.

23. Sten Konow, "Mathura Brāhmī Inscription of the year 28", *E.I.*, XXI, pp. 55-61.

24. D.C. Sircar, "Mathura Stone Inscription of Huviṣka — (Śaka) year 28", *Select Inscriptions*, pp. 151-52, pl. XXVII.

25. I am thankful to A.K. Srivastava, the Director of the Museum, for providing facilities to examine the inscription and also to Pushpa Thukrail, the Deputy Director, for taking me to the old Museum Building, where the inscription is stored.

26. For instance, Vaśiṣka Kuṣāṇa is shortened in the Sāñchī Inscription as *Vasakuṣāṇa* (referred to above). Another instance is seen in a Kankali Tilā Jain Image, now in the Lucknow Museum. There Huviṣka is written as *Huṣka* (G. Bühler, "Further Jain Inscriptions from Mathura", *E.I.*, II, p. 206.

27. D.R. Sahni, "Seven Inscriptions from Mathura", *E.I.,* XIX, p. 66, no. 3.
28. B.N. Mukherjee, *The Kuṣāṇa Genealogy,* Calcutta, 1967, pp. 75-77.
29. Kankali Tilā Jain Image, Lucknow Museum, G. Bühler, New Jain Inscriptions from Mathura, *E.I.,* p. 391, no. 19.
30. Kankali Tilā Jain Image, R.D. Banerjee, "New Brāhmī Inscriptions of the Scythian Period", *Ibid.,* X, p. 109, no. 3.
31. Buddhist Pedestal, Mathura Museum, D.R. Sahni, Mathura Pedestal Inscription of the Kaniṣka year 14, *ibid,* p. 96-97.
32. Kankali Tilā Jain Image, Mathura Museum, Rosenfield, *op. cit.,* p. 271.
33. Mentioned above footnotes 29 and 32.
34. Original paper was submitted to the Colloquium on the Later Kuṣāṇa Numismatics held at London on November 5 and 6, 1981.

11

Kuṣāṇa Coins from Mathura Region*

A CAREFUL scrutiny of the coins that are found in Mathura region reveals no trace of Kujūla Kadphises, the first Kuṣāṇa ruler. It means that he had no hold in this region. According to Cunningham, the coins of Soter Megas were found at Mathura and in almost all the places in Madhyadeśa along with the coins of the Great Kuṣāṇas. He also detected a local type of his coins at Mathura.[1] But we have not found a single coin of Soter Megas of any type in the course of our investigations of coins current at Mathura. We are disinclined to attach importance to what Cunningham has said. We feel that Vima Kadphises was the first Kuṣāṇa ruler who occupied Mathura after the Kṣatrapas. If twenty years is assigned to his reign in Mathura, his date would then be in the second or third decade of the second century A.D.

At this stage, a copper coin attracts our attention. It was found on the surface at Sonkh during the excavations in the area of the Nāga apsidal temple, outside the main excavation site. Immediately under the temple lay an early Kuṣāṇa structure.[2] The copper coin has Brāhmī legends on both the faces. On one face, the legend is clearly *Huviṣkasya* in one line; on the other face, the legend is in two lines and may be read as *putra ka/ ṇaka(sya)* (*fig. 2*). The division of a legend on the two faces of a coin is probably unknown anywhere in Indian numismatics;

* Originally submitted to the Colloquium on Mathura: The Cultural Heritage organised by the American Institute of Indian Studies at New Delhi, in 1980. *Mathura: The Cultural Heritage*, (ed. D.M. Srinivasan), New Delhi1989, pp. 132-135.

but here the legends can be read meaningfully only when they are taken together and read as *Huviṣkasya putra Kaṇikasya.* It would then mean that the Kaṇika was the issuer of the coin and he was the son of Huviṣka.[3] We do not know of Kaniṣka, who was the son of Huviṣka. It may be said that Huviṣka, whom, we know as the successor of Kaniṣka, might have had a son named Kaniṣka. But on this coin, we see no device which could be called Kuṣāṇian. Here the human figure, though wearing a foreign dress, is unlike the figures of the king or the deity, seen on Kuṣāṇa coins. The figure is closer to the figures seen on the early indigenous coins.[3a] The coin is un-Kuṣāṇian also in fabric and execution. The obverse device with a square incuse is the feature of early Indian numismatics. It is known at the latest on the coins of the Pañcāla series that had ended with the advent of the Kuṣāṇas. Moreover, no regal title, which is known on the Kuṣāṇa coins, is used here either for Huviṣka or for Kaniṣka; and no Kuṣāṇa king had ever used patronymic on their coins, where as this is seen on the coins of Mathura Kṣatrapa Śoḍāsa (*Rājuvulaputasa Khatapasa Śoḍāsasa*).[3b] These peculiarites make it almost certain that the coin belongs to a very early period in the Kuṣāṇa history at Mathura. From the point of palaeography also, the coin does not seem to be of any later date than Kaniṣka I. The name Kaṇika is used in literature only for Kaniṣka I.[4] This means that the coin was issued only for him in the very early period of his entry into Mathura in keeping with the local traditions. His coins with Graeco-Bactrian script might have been issued later and for circulation in his entire dominion. This coin thus brings to light an unknown fact that Kaṇika (Kaniṣka I) was the son of Huviṣka (whom we may call Huviṣka I).

That Kaniṣka's father, Huviṣka I, had succeeded Vima Kadphises is indicated from a few gold coins, which have so far been attributed to the Huviṣka who succeeded Kaniṣka I. It was never seriously taken that the coins bearing the name Huviṣka were the coins of more than one person of the same name. It is not that the idea of two Huviṣkas is new. Earlier, it was suggested by F.W. Thomas[5], A.L. Basham,[6] A.K. Narain[7] and S.K. Maity[8] on various considerations. We are not concerned here with most of the arguments adduced by them. I would refer only to two different spellings of the name Huviṣka—*Oeṣko* (*OOHÞKO*) and *Oeṣki* (*OOHÞKI*), on the basis of which Narain has postulated two Huviṣkas.[9] He did not rely merely on the difference in the spelling of the name but also cited a parallel instance to substantiate it. He pointed out that the name of Kaniṣka I on his coins is spelled as *Kaneṣki* (*KANHÞKI*) and it is *Kaneṣko* (*KANHÞKO*) on the coins that are later and attributed to Kaniṣka III. The reasons for two different spellings could only be the differentiation between two rulers of the same name. If that were true in the case of Kaniṣka, it would well be true in the case of Huviṣka, also.

In addition, I would like to add that the spelling *Oeṣko* (*OOHÞKO*) is seen only on two varieties of coins: (1) the Elephant-rider[10] and (2) King seated cross-legged.[11] On all the other coins having the bust of the king, the spelling uniformly is *Oeṣki* (*OOHÞKI*). The cross-legged royal portraits go back to the days of Maues, Azes II and Kujūla Kadphises;[12] and the elephant type is similar to that of Vima Kadphises.[13] These types are quite unknown in the coin-series of Kaniṣka I, who intervened between Vima Kadphises and Huviṣka (Huviṣka II of my reckoning). This could not be termed mere accident. Again, the forms of the monograms on the coins of these two types, is the same as is seen on the coins of Vima Kadphises () (*fig. 7*) and Kaniṣka; Huviṣka's own monogram was () (*fig. 8*), which is seen exclusively on the bust-type coins. The types, the monogram and the spelling, when taken together, isolate the issuer of the Elephant-rider and Cross-legged types from the issuer of the bust-type coins. These coin types indicate that the issuer of the former two types was earlier than Kaniṣka I and close to Vima Kadphises and was distinct from that Huviṣka who issued coins with the bust type and who came after Kaniṣka I.

Here it might be of interest to mention that D.W. MacDowall has analyzed the weights of the copper coins, attributed to Huviṣka[14] and has detected two distinct chronological groups on the basis of a striking decrease in weight standard and the change in the monogram. According to him, the first group of Huviṣka's copper coins are those that have the obverse legend commencing at I o'clock and have the well-made form of the reverse symbol, which is the same as that used by Vima Kadphises and Kaniṣka () (*fig. 7*). The coins of the first group show the king riding on an elephant, sitting cross-legged and seated on a couch. These coins show a clear point of concentration at 15-16 grammes, representing the tetradrachm denomination of Vima Kadphises and Kaniṣka. The second group of Huviṣka's copper coins is characterized by the use of a distinct symbol () (*fig. 8*), seen also on the bust-type gold coins. It is generally engraved with a reasonable amount of care. The legend on these coins does not commence at one o'clock and the letters are larger and less well-formed. These coins range between 8 and 13 grammes, and were struck to a standard of 10 to 12 grammes.

MacDowall had been cautious about the interpretation of the significance of the apparent division; he, therefore, suggested the possibility of two separate stages in the issues of these coins or separate mint-centers. But in view of the distinctions noticed in the gold coins discussed above, it may now be reasonably said that the two divisions in the copper coins also lead to the same conclusion as derived from the gold coins, viz. there was more than one Huviṣka, and one of them may well be placed between Vima Kadphises and Kaniṣka I. This Huviṣka (i.e., Huviṣka I) may well be identified with the Huviṣka mentioned on the copper coins found at Sonkh.

Again, the bust-type gold coins of Huviṣka may well be divided into two groups indicating that they were the issues of not one but two rulers named Huviṣka (i.e., Huviṣka II and III). While these coins uniformly show the king holding a mace or club in his right hand, the object in his left hand helps distiguish the coins into two varieties. On some coins, he holds an *aṅkuśa*[15] (goad) (*fig. 9*), and on the other a spear or scepter[16] (*fig. 10)*. I suggest that they relate to two distinct rulers of the same name. Without going into any detail to substantiate the suggestion, it would suffice to cite the parallel instance of the coins of Azes

I and II. G.K. Jenkins distinguished two Azeses on the basis of the object held by the horse-rider in his hand. Jenkins pointed out that Azes I held a spear and Azes II had a whip.[17] (*figs. 11 & 13*)

That the above-mentioned two types of the coins belonged to two Huviṣkas (II and III) is substantiated from two hoards of gold coins discovered in Uttar Pradesh. One of them found in 1965 in the district of Barabanki had thirteen coins, all are of Huviṣka and are exclusively of the type where the king holds *aṅkuśa* (goad); the hoard included none of the type where he holds a spear or a sceptre.[18] The other hoard that was discovered in the district of Garhwal in 1971 had forty-five coins — forty-four of Huviṣka and one of Vāsudeva. Here all the forty-four coins of Huviṣka were of the type where the king holds a sceptre. On none of them he is seen holding *aṅkuśa*[19] (goad). The two hoards are so distinct in their contents that they unmistakably mean that the two types of the coins were separately issued in two different periods. The association of the coin of Vāsudeva in the Garhwal hoard, makes it certain that the spear-type coins were later.[20] This *aṅkuśa*-type coins belonged to Huviṣka II and the sceptre-type of Huviṣka III.

Here reference may again be made to MacDowall's observations about the weights of Huviṣka's copper coins. He has distinguished the copper coins of group II, mentioned above, into two classes, on the basis of their weights. They represent the standard (1) 10 to 20 grammes and (2) 7 to 9 grammes. He places them into two distinct chronological phases.[21] They may well be the coins of two successive rulers of the same name.

The inscriptions bearing the name of Huviṣka are known to cover quite a long period of time, from Kaniṣka years 28 to 60.[22] This may well be the period of two Huviṣkas (II and III). During this period whether the two Huviṣkas were successive rulers or someone had intervened between them remains to be investigated.

Huviṣka (III) was succeeded by Vāsudeva. This is clear from the Garhwal hoard, just mentioned above. His inscriptions of the

Kaniṣka years 64 (or 67) to 98 years are known from Mathura region[23] and they testify to his existence there. The political history of the Mathura region after him is obscure. The Yaudheyas and/ or the Nāgas are vaguely considered as responsible for the decline of the Kuṣāṇa rule in this region. But hardly any coin of the Yaudheyas can be seen in the Mathura Museum and the Nāga coins there are also so few[24] that they are insufficient to suggest any kind of occupation at Mathura. As such, there has been vacuum in the history of Mathura from this time till the rise of the Guptas.

Some information about this period of history may be elicited from the coin-hoards known from Uttar Pradesh and the vicinity. But no proper attention has so far been given to them. A close scrutiny of the hoards of copper coins[25] indicates that they are distinguishable into two clear groups. One group of these hoards, known from all parts of Kuṣāṇa dominion, includes only the coins of the earlier Kuṣāṇa rulers (Vima Kadphises to Huviṣka). In them the Vāsudeva coins are generally absent; in a few cases where his coins have been found, their number is too small to be of any value. The other group of the hoards are exclusively the coins of Vāsudeva and his successors, and these hoards of copper coins are confined in and around Mathura region. Only the hoards of the gold coins have a little wider diffusion. This division of the hoards, by itself, is very significant. It makes it clear that by the time of Vāsudeva, or in the early part of his reign, the Kuṣāṇa domain had greatly diminished in the east. It had become limited to the Mathura region and its periphery. It was not wiped out, as is generally believed.

The copper coins of the second group found in and around Mathura[26] would have been the best evidence for our purpose, but unfortunately, they have never been properly studied and published. However, five gold coin hoards, known to me, though not found exactly in the Mathura region, may serve our purpose well. One of them came from the District of Jaunpur and had thirty-three coins,[27] the other hoard had only twelve coins and was found in Unao District;[28] the third hoard had twenty-one coins and was found in Meerut District.[29] All these Districts lay in Uttar Pradesh, the great part of which was under the influence of the Kuṣāṇas and was governed from Mathura. The fourth hoard of ten coins was discovered in the village Dado Fatehpur, Khetri (District Jhunjhunu, Rajasthan).[30] The fifth hoard was found at Mithathal in the District of Hisar (Haryana Pradesh).[31] Both these places are not very far from the Mathura region.

The contents of these five hoards of gold coins, when studied together, present a link between the Kuṣāṇa Vāsudeva I at one end and Samudragupta of the Gupta dynasty at the other end, with an unbroken chain of at least five rulers — Vāsudeva II, Kaniṣka III, Bazeṣka (Vaśiṣka), Vasu and Ṣaka.[32] They thus show that there was no hiatus at any time in the period between the Kuṣāṇas and the Guptas. This, however, does not mean that Ṣaka, whose coins are known in the Mithathal hoard, was the ruler of the Mathura region or was a necessarily a Kuṣāṇa ruler.[33] It only indicates a chronological sequence of the rulers up to the time of the rise of the Guptas under Samudragupta.

We have plenty of copper coins at Mathura in the continued tradition of the Ardokṣo reverse type coins of Kaniṣka III and Vāsudeva II. They indicate that a few more rulers might have existed in the chain of the Kuṣāṇa rulers in the Mathura region. Three types of such coins are illustrated here (*figs. 26-28*). Of them, one is most interesting (*fig. 26*). Here the king is seated on a throne, facing front, holding a fillet *(pāśa)* in the right hand and with the left hand upraised, probably holding a staff. Behind his right hand is a pointed spear of broad blade replacing the trident of the earlier coins of Vasu and others. To the right of the right hand, below the arm appears a legend *Vīra*. Perhaps, below the left hand are also a few letters, which are not clear. This coin undoubtedly belongs to a king named Vīra, probably a successor of Vasu. The other two coins might be later issues.

In the light of the above, we may have a hundred years after Vāsudeva I for Vāsudeva II, Kaniṣka II, Vasu, Vīra and a few other rulers that might have succeeded Vasu or intervened between these rulers. It may now be said that the Kuṣāṇa rule terminated only with the rise of Samudragupta. Samudragupta's date may well be placed in about 350 A.D. As such, the date of these post-Vāsudeva rulers might have commenced around 250 A.D. If we accept this date for the Kaniṣka year 98, the last known date for Vāsudeva I, the commencement of the Kaniṣka era would then be around 140-150 A.D., almost the same, as was suggested by me earlier.[34]

References

1. A Cunningham, *Coins of the Sakas,* Part II, p. 14; 55 (compiled in *Coins of the Indo-Scythians, Sakas and Kuṣāṇas,* Varanasi, 1971, Reprint). Cunningham says that these coins are not found elsewhere; but Whitehead had found them in Delhi and Jagadhari. He says that probably they were current in south-east Punjab (*P.M.C.,* p. 162, fn. 1).
2. Härtel does not mention this coin in his *Report.* However, I have published it ('A Kuṣāṇa Coin with Brāhmī Legend', *J.N.S.I.,* XXXV [1973], pp. 123-28); See supra pp. 65-70.
3. If the legends on the two sides are interpreted independently as Härtel suggested during the discussion on this paper, and *putra Kaṇikasya* is taken to mean 'son of Kaniṣka', then Huviṣka may be regarded as the issuer of the coin. But this interpretation would be most unusual. To mean 'son of Kaniṣka', the correct form would be *Kaṇikasya putra* and never *putra Kaṇikasya.*

3a. Compare with the figure on Ujjayini coins (*B.M.C.,A.I.,* pl. XXXVII, 1-4.

3b. *B.M.C.,A.I.,* p. 191, var. *b.*

4. For the identification of Kaṇika with Kaniṣka I, see B.N. Mukherjee, *The Kuṣānas and the Deccan,* Calcutta, 1968, p. 27; 40; 45 fn. 19; 49 fn. 51; 50; fn. 52; B. N. Mukherjee, *The Kuṣāṇa Genealogy,* Calcutta, 1967, p. 116, fn. 180; also S. Levi, 'Notes on the Indo-Scythians', *I.A.,* XXXII (1903), pp. 380-89. F.W. Thomas, *Tibetan Literary Texts and Documents concerning Chinese Turkistan,* London, 1935, p. 119 fn 2; W.H. Rockhill, *The Life of Buddha,* p. 280, fn. 2.
5. F. W. Thomas, 'Notes on the Scythian Period', *J.R.A.S.,* 1952, p. 116.
6. A.L. Basham, 'The Succession of the Line of Kaniṣka', *B.S.O.A.S.,* XX (1957), pp. 77-78.
7. A.K. Narain, 'A Unique Gold and Two Silver Coins of Huviṣka', *J.N.S.I.,* XXII (1960), p. 99.
8. S.K. Maity, 'The Gold Content of the Kuṣāṇa, Kuṣāṇa chiefs and the

Sassanian Gold Coins from the Indian Museum, Calcutta', *J.N.S.I.*, XX (1958), p. 164; 166.

9. To reject this suggestion, B.N. Mukherjee has pointed out to the rules of grammer, laid down for the Bactrian language, to show that both the forms were valid for the same name (*The Kuṣāṇa Genealogy*, pp. 66-67). But grammar does not overrule common sense. Common sense is that no one writes or spells his name in two different forms. If the two forms of the same are used, it unmistakably means that they do not mean one and the same person.
10. J.M. Rosenfield, *The Dynastic Arts of the Kuṣāṇas*, Los Angeles, 1967, p. 61; Pl. III, 41-42.
11. *Ibid.*, p. 62; Pl. III, 44.
12. *Ibid.*, p. 14; Pl. I, 6.
13. *Ibid.*, p. 22; Pl. I, 17. It is noteworthy that a coin of this type was found at Varanasi (H. H. Wilson, *Ariana Indica*, p. 354).
14. D.W. MacDowall, 'The Weight Standards of the Gold and Copper Coinages of the Kuṣāṇa Dynasty from Vima-Kadphises to Vasudeva', *J.N.S.I.*, XXII (1960), pp. 71-73.
15. Rosenfield, *Dynastic Arts*, p. 63; Pl. III, pp. 48-59.
16. *Ibid.*, p. 84; Pl. III, 60; IV, 61-74.
17. G.K. Jenkins, 'Indo-Scythic Mints', *J.N.S.I.*, XVII (1955), pp. 1-2.
18. A.K. Srivastava, 'Kuṣāna Gold Coins from Barabanki District', *J.N.S.I.*, XXXI (1969), pp. 15-21.
19. A.K. Srivastava, 'Kuṣāṇa Coins from Tehri-Garhwal', *J.N.S.I.*, XXXVIII (1975), pp. 72-73.
20. A hoard of gold coins, found in the Meerut District (Unpublished in State Museum, Lucknow); also shows that sceptre-type coins of Huviṣka were later. This hoard included a coin of Huviṣka along with those of Vāsudeva and his successors. Unfortunately, the coin of Huviṣka of this hoard is not traceable now. But from its description, given in the *Treasure Trove Report*, available in the State Museum, Lucknow, it was a rare type coin showing the king wearing a turban in the Indian style. This coin might have been similar to the coin in the State Museum, Münich (West Germany) (A.K. Narain, 'A Unique Gold and Two Silver coin of Huviṣka' *J.N.S.I.*, XXII [1960], p. 7). the Münich coin shows that the king holds a sceptre in his right hand.
21. D. W. MacDowall, *op. cit.*, pp. 71-72.
22. Rosenfield, *Dynastic Arts*, pp. 226-68.
23. *Ibid.*, pp. 268-70.

24. Just before the preparation of this paper, the Mathura Museum Coin Collection and a private collection at Mathura were thoroughly examined by me.

25. List of the finds of the Kuṣāṇa coins in Bihar, Bengal and Orissa and the adjoining areas is given in my paper 'Kuṣāṇa-Muruṇḍa Rule in Eastern India', *J.N.S.I.,* XXXVI (1974), pp. 29-39; (supra pp. 71-102). My two earlier papers include the finds from Eastern Uttar Pradesh ('Eastern Expansion of the Kuṣāṇa Empire', *I.H.Q.,* XXIX [1953], pp. 212-14; (supra, pp. 21-40) 'The Date of Kuṣāṇa Currency in Eastern India', *J.N.S.I.,* XV [1953], pp. 185-89); (supra, pp. 41-50). List of the finds of the Kuṣāṇa coins in U.P. has also been prepared by C.S. Srivastava and A.K. Srivastava based on the Treasure Trove Reports (*B.M.A.,U.P.,* nos. 3 and 8, 1969 and 1971, respectively).

26. A hoard of 1221 coins was found at Māṭ. Another hoard of 120 coins was discovered in the excavations at Sonkh (A.K. Srivastava, 'Findspots of Kuṣāna Coins in U.P.' (*B.M.A.U.P.,* no. 8 (1971), p. 40, Entries 15 and 17). Recently, a third hoard of about 1500 coins was found at Govindnagar (Now in Mathura Museum. Information A.K. Srivastava). A fourth hoard of 296 coins was found at Jamba Ranger in Jaipur District (Rajasthan) not very far from the Mathura region (probably now in Jaipur Museum. Information, Premlata Pokhama).

27. A.K. Srivastava, 'A Hoard of Kuṣāṇa Coins from Jaunpur district', *B.M.A.U.P.,* no. 4, 1966, pp. 27-30. According to Srivastava, it included the coins of Kaniṣka, Vāsudeva, Kaniṣka III and Vasu. But on one of the coins B.N. Mukherjee has found the name *Bazeṣko* clearly written ('A Gold Coin of Bazeshko', *J.N.S.I.,* XXXIV [1972], pp. 31-35). This adds a new name to the list of the later Kuṣāṇa rulers. He may perhaps be identified with Vaśiṣka or Vaskuṣāṇa of the Sanchi inscriptions (J. Marshall, A. Foucher, and N.G. Majumdar, *The Monuments of Sanchi,* three volumes, Calcutta, 1940, pp. 385-86) which bear the dates 28 and 22 respectively and are reckoned in the second Kuṣāṇa era by some scholars. See also supra, pp. 136.

28. A. K. Srivastava, 'Kuṣāṇa Gold Coins from Unnao District', *B.M.A.U.P.,* nos. 5-6 (1970), pp. 31-32. It includes post-Vāsudeva coins.

29. *Indian Archaeology,* 1953-54, p. 39. 'The information given here is vague and to some extent inaccurate. There was no Kuṣāṇo-Sassanian coin in the hoard. I had examined this hoard at the Lucknow Museum. It contained one coin of Huviṣka (king holding spear); six coins of Vāsudeva (plain type 2; scyphate type 6; five coins of Kaniṣka (Śiva and Bull type) and ten coins of Kaniṣka III (Ardokṣo type).

30. P. Pokharna, 'A Hoard of Kuṣāṇa gold coins from Rajasthan', *J.N.S.I.,* XXXIX (1977), p. 160; *N.D.,* V II, 1981, pp. 25-35.

31. The hoard was found in 1915 and still is unpublished. Originally it had eighty-six coins; but only sixty coins came into official hands. Of them, thirty-three belonged to the Imperial Guptas (twenty-nine of Samudragupta and four of Kācagupta) and the rest related to the Kuṣāṇas. Till recently, the only information about the hoards was that it included a coin of the Battle-axe type of Samudragupta, a rare variety (*A.S.I.,A.R.*, 1915-16, p. 25; 1926-27, p. 19; A. S. Altekar, *Coinage of the Gupta Empire*, Varanasi, 1957, p. 309). Later I had an occasion to lay hands on the *Annual Reports* of the Central Museum, Lahore. The *Report* for the year 1915-16 disclosed that the hoard was originally examined by R.B. Whitehead and he had then prepared a very brief note on it. According to his note, the notable coins in the hoard were: a very fine piece of Samudragupta's Battle-axe type, a coin of Samudragupta's *Aśvamedha* type and four coins of Kācagupta. He did not say a word about the Kuṣāṇa contents. However, the *Report* for the year 1916-17 disclosed that twenty coins from this hoard (eleven of the Guptas and nine of the Kuṣāṇas) were acquired by the Museum. The *Report* has illustrated all the twenty coins but without any description. The illustrations reveal that the Museum's acquisition included two coins of Vāsudeva (Śiva-Nandi reverse), two coins of Kaniṣka II (Śiva-Nandi reverse), two coins of Kaniṣka III (Ardokṣo reverse), two coins of Vasu (Ardokṣo reverse) and one coin of *Ṣaka* (Ardokṣo reverse). In the light of this disclosure, it may well be presumed that the remaining coins, that were not acquired by the Museum, would have been the duplicates of these coins. Thus we now have a fair idea of the hoard.
32. To have a clear historical picture, these hoards need a detailed treatment and a critical study. Whatever has been said here is the sum substance of the hoard study.
33. P.L. Gupta, *The Imperial Guptas*, Varanasi, 1974, p. 250.
34. Infra, p. 183.

12

Kuṣāṇas in the Yamuno-Gangetic Region*

A NOMADIC tribe, known to the Chinese sources as Yueh-chi, had left their homeland on the Chinese border early in *circa* second century B.C. and arrived in the Oxus region and settled at Bactria. After having dwelt there for about a century, a prince of the Kue-Shang branch of the Yueh-chi invaded Parthia or the parts of the Indo-Parthian realm in Afghanistan, occupied Central Afghanistan, Gandhāra and the lower Swat Valley. His successors came to be known as the Kuṣāṇas. They spread their kingdom up to the Yamuno-Gangetic region into Northern India; and had thus built a great empire that extended up to Vārāṇasī in the east.

Much has been said about the history of these Kuṣāṇas, mostly based on the Chinese sources and the archaeological remains found in the western part of their empire — Afghanistan and Central Asia. The basic Indian sources, particularly from the Yamuno-Gangetic region have remained mostly neglected.

An attempt is made here to assess the history of the Kuṣāṇas, as gleaned from the inscriptions and coins, found in this region, particularly those that have come to light in recent years.

Leaving aside the few rulers that existed at the very beginning and were confined to the western region in and around Bactria, the Kuṣāṇas are generally identified into two distinct

---

* Originally published in *Annali* (Instituto Universitario Orientale), Naples, Italy, 45 (1985), pp. 199-222.

groups. One group, the earlier one, consisted of only two rulers — Kuzūla Kadphises and Vima Kadphises. The second group is said to have its beginning with the king named Kaniṣka. The rulers of this latter group existed for several generations; and their history is the main history of the Kuṣāṇas.

Vima Kadphises in The East

We have neither any inscription nor coins of the first ruler of the first group — Kuzūla Kadphises from anywhere in the eastern part of the Kuṣāṇa empire, i.e., Yamuno-Gangetic region. It is very well apparent that he did not come into this area. It is only the second ruler, Vima Kadphises, whose coins are found in this area to suggest his existence; but no inscription was so far known for him. Lately, a Brāhmī inscription, engraved on a Śiva-liṅga have come to light from a place called Reh in the Fatehpur district of Uttar Pradesh, situated on the bank of the Yamunā (*fig. 31*), which may be related to him.

The lower portion of this inscription is broken and missing. Only three lines are preserved; they have been read by G.R. Sharma, the discoverer, as follows:

1. *Mahārājasa Rājarājasa*
2. *Mahaṁtasa trātārasa dhaṁmi-*
3. *kasa jayaṁtasa ca apra*

There are also the remnants of the fourth line below, which has been conjecturally restored by Sharma as *[jitasa] Minanda(de?)rasa*. With this restoration, he has attributed this inscription to the Indo-Greek ruler Menander. In this inscription, he has found a corroborative evidence for the 'valliantly wicked Yavanas marching along Mathura to Pāṭaliputra'.[1]

In restoring the line Sharma has not considered the palaeography with any seriousness. His conjecture about the fourth line, as having the name of Menander, is based merely on the assumption that the titles, mentioned in the first three lines, given to the king, are the Prākṛt translation of the Greek

Basileos basileon megalou soteros dikaiou kai aniketou Menandrou. Placing this interesting interpretation, Sharma has failed to realise the basic fact that *Basileos Basileon* was never used by any Indo-Greek king, either on their coins or inscriptions. This title came into vogue in India only during the time of the Śaka-Pahlava rulers. They had used this title on their coins. Of the other titles, mentioned in the inscription, only *tratara* and *dhramika* are the two, known on Menander's coins; and there too, they were never used together. The other titles were individually used by other Indo-Greek rulers on their coins. They are not known at one place, anywhere used for any Indo-Greek king. On the other hand, as has been pointed out by T.P. Verma,[2] all the Prākṛt titles, used in the inscription, were used together, in this very form, on an inscription found at Kamra in North-western Afghanistan for a Kuṣāṇa ruler.[3] These facts make it absolutely clear that the Reh Inscription does not relate in any way to Menander. His name cannot be made out in the remnants of the latter part of the fourth line of the inscription by any flight of imagination. The inscription can only be related to an early Kuṣāṇa ruler; and he would only be Vima Kadphises, whose coins are found in this region. A clay sealing, bearing his name, has recently been found at Piprahwā in Basti district, Uttar Pradesh.[4] His expedition to the east is testified by the Hāthīgumphā Inscription.[5]

Huviṣka I–Father of Kaniṣka

It is a common belief that Vima Kadphises was succeeded by Kaniṣka, the first ruler of the second group. In what way this Kaniṣka was related to Vima Kadphises; or whether Kaniṣka occupied the Yamuno-Gangetic region immediately after Vima or there was any gap between the two, are a few questions in the Kuṣāṇa history, which remain still unanswered.

At this point, a copper coin (*fig. 2*) attracts our attention. This coin was found at Sonkh in Mathura district during an archaeological expedition led by Herbert Härtel. It was found on the surface in the area of a Nāga apsidal temple, immediately under which lay the early Kuṣāṇa structures. The coin bears Brāhmī legend on both the faces. On one face the legend is clear *Huviṣkasya* in one line; on the other face the legend is in two lines and may reasonably be read as *putra ka/ṇika[sya]*. The legend on two sides, when put together, would be read as *Huviṣkasya putra Kaṇikasya* and would mean that Kaṇika was the issuer of the coin and he was the son of Huviṣka.

Since we do not know so far any Kaniṣka, who was the son of Huviṣka and the only Huviṣka, whom we know, was the successor of Kaniṣka, it may *prima facie* be assumed, on the basis of this coin, that Huviṣka, the successor of Kaniṣka, had a son, who was known as Kaniṣka (Kaṇika). But a careful examination rules out this possibility. The coin bears no device which could be called Kuṣāṇian. The human figure, though it wears a foreign dress, is unlike the effigies of any king or deity, seen on the Kuṣāṇa coins. He is more close to the figures seen on the early indigenous coins.[6] In fabric and execution also, the coin is un-Kuṣāṇian. The square incuse, which is here on the obverse was the feature of the early Indian numismatics. It is known late on the coins of the Pañcāla series, which ended almost with the advent of the Kuṣāṇas in the Gangetic plains. Moreover, no regal title, which is known on the Kuṣāṇa coins, is used here for either Huviṣka or Kaniṣka. While the absence of ragal titles was well prevalent on the early Indian coins. Again, no Kuṣāṇa king had ever used any kind of patronymia, where as it may well be seen on the coins of Kṣatrāpa Sodāṣa, the ruler of Mathura. We have the legend there - Rājuvulaputasa Khatapasa Śoḍāsasa? These peculiarities indicate that the coin belonged to a very early state of the Kuṣāṇa emergence in the Yamuno-Gangetic region. It followed the local numismatic traditions that was current in this area. From the point of palaeography also, the coin does not seem to be of any later date than Kaniṣka I; and Kaniṣka I is the only king, who is known in the literary traditions as Kanika. This coin was, most likely, issued earlier, before the coins of Kaniṣka I of the usual type were introduced here with the Graeco-Bactrian script. This coin thus, adds to our knowledge that Kaṇika (Kaniṣka I) was the son of Huviṣka, who may be designated as

Huviṣka I to distinguish him from the later Huviṣka, the successor of Kaniṣka I. This coin also makes it clear that Vima Kadphises might not have immediately succeeded by Kaniṣka I; or at least that Kaniṣka I was not the immediate descendant of Vima Kadphises.

This fact that Kaniṣka I was the son of Huviṣka I, finds support in the pedestal inscription, found at Māṭ (Mathura).[6] This inscription is mutilated and occasionally obscure; but the form in which it is restored, shows that a *devakula* (shrine of ancestors) was established by one or for one, who is called *satyadharmasthita*; but his name is mutilated. Nevertheless, it is clear that he was not Kuzūla Kadphises, who is known by this title, as this title here is preceded by the letters *mārasya,* which may be restored as *kumārasya*. It further adds to our knowledge that an image of *Mahārāja rājatirāja Huviṣka pitāmaha,* along with a tank was established there. The *devakula* was depleted; so, for the *āyur-balavṛddhi of Mahārāja rajatirāja devaputra Huviṣka,* some *mahādaṇḍanāyaka* got it repaired. Here *Huviṣka pitāmaha* is generally interpreted as 'the grand-father of Huviṣka'. With this interpretation, the name of the grand-father is found missing; so, it is suggested that it meant Vima Kadphises, who is identified with Vematakṣama — a name, which is found on another pedestal inscription found at this very site of Māṭ.[9]

Unfortunately, in interpreting the line in this way, the basic fact is not realised that the two inscriptions belonged to two different statues, on whose pedestals they are engraved. Both the statues would not have been of the same person. It is not expected to have more than one statue of any ancestor in any *devakula. Huviṣka pitāmaha* would never be Vematakṣama, even if he be identified with Vima Kadphises.[10]

It is quite evident, thus, that *Huviṣka pitāmaha* in the Māṭ Inscription would not have meant in any way Vima Kadphises. Actually the term, as has been pointed out by F.W. Thomas[11] and supported by Bussagli,[12] never meant 'grand-father of Huviṣka'; its simple and natural interpretation would be 'Huviṣka the elder (or the grandfather)'. The epithet *pitāmaha* (the elder) is used here to distinguish Huviṣka, whose statue was installed on the pedestal from Huviṣka, the reigning monarch. His inscription clearly brings out the fact that there was one Huviṣka, earlier than that Huviṣka, with whom we all are familiar.

Apart from this inscription, we have the testimony of the *Rājataraṅgiṇī* of Kalhaṇa. He has mentioned three rulers named Huṣka, Juṣka and Kaniṣka, who are said to have founded three cities after their own names.[13] Since the historicity of Kalhaṇa's statement cannot be denied, it undoubtedly means that two rulers, named Huṣka and Juṣka had preceded Kaniṣka. While we do not know anything about Juṣka as yet, Huṣka may conveniently be identified as Huviṣka. It need not say that Huṣka was a short form of the name Huviṣka, as appears from an inscription from Mathura.[14] This means that a Huviṣka had preceded Kaniṣka.

That one Huviṣka had succeeded Vima Kadphises is also indicated by some gold coins. On the basis of the gold coins, that bear the name Huviṣka the existence of two Huviṣkas has already been suggested by F.W. Thomas,[15] A.L. Basham,[16] A.K. Narain,[17] and S.K. Maity[18] but in a different context. What is relevant here is that A.K. Narain has pointed out to two different spellings of the name Huviṣka; it is *Oeṣko* on some coins and *Oeṣkī* on others. He drew attention to the fact that the name of Kaniṣka I is always spelt as *Kaneṣki* on his coins, and it is spelt as *Kaneṣko* on the coins that are attributed to a later Kaniṣka — Kaniṣka III. The two different spellings of the name Kaniṣka clearly meant to differentiate between the two rulers of the same name; similarly the difference in the spelling of the name Huviṣka on the coins would have the same connotation. What is true in the case of the former, would also be true in the case of the latter.

Narain's argument is perfectly sound; but he has missed to realise the most important fact, which is very much significant and relevant in the present context. It is that the spelling *Oeṣko* is seen on only two types of the gold coins of Huviṣka; (i) the elephant-rider (*fig. 3*) and (ii) king seated cross-legged (*fig. 4*).

On all the other coins of Huviṣka that are uniformly of the bust type, the spelling is *Oeṣkī*. The coins of both the types bearing the name *Oeṣko*, are equally known of Vima Kadphises (*figs. 5-6*). But both these types are conspicuously absent in the coin series of Kaniṣka I who intervened between Vima Kadphises and Huviṣka (Huviṣka II). This would not simply be an accident. The monogram on the reverse of the coins of these two types of Huviṣka is the same as seen on the coins of Vima Kadphises and Kaniṣka () (*fig. 7*). Thus not only the spelling of the name but also the types of the coins and their monogram isolate the coins of Huviṣka into two groups and show that they belong to two Huviṣkas. It may convincingly be said that the elephant-rider and cross-legged types of coins were issued by the Huviṣka (Huviṣka I), who was close to Vima Kadphises and was earlier than Kaniṣka I; and he was different from Huviṣka, who succeeded Kaniṣka I and issued bust type coins.

This conclusion, deduced from the gold coins, is supported also by the copper coins attributed to Huviṣka. D.W. MacDowall has analysed them and detected in them two distinct chronological groups based on the striking decrease in the weight standard and in the change of the reverse monogram.[19] According to his analysis, the first group of Huviṣka's copper coins is that that has on the obverse the legend commencing at 1 o'clock and have the well made form of the reverse monogram, which is the same as used by Vima Kadphises and Kaniṣka (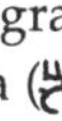) (*fig. 7*). These coins show the king riding on elephant, sitting cross-legged and seated on couch. They show a clear point of concentration at 15-16 grammes, representing the tetradrachm denomination of Vima Kadphises and Kaniṣka. The second group of Huviṣka's copper coins is characterised by the use of a quite distinct monogram () (*fig. 8*). The legend on these coins does not commence at 1 o'clock and the letters are larger and less well formed. These coins range between 8 and 13 grammes and were struck to a standard of 10 to 12 grammes. These two divisions of the copper coins, represent the coins of two different periods, was the conclusion of MacDowall.[20] All these evidences, put together, show that there were two Huviṣkas, one was close to Vima

Kadphises and the other was that who succeeded Kaniṣka I. And to this the Sonkh copper coin adds to our knowledge that Huviṣka I was the father of Kaniṣka I.

Huviṣka II and III

A large number of Brāhmī inscriptions, bearing the names of the Kuṣāṇa rulers are known from Mathura and the surroundings. They are dated from year 2 to 98 of an unspecified era, which has been assumed to be the Kaniṣka or Kuṣāṇa era. They disclose the reign of Kaniṣka I from the year 2[21] to 23[22] and of Huviṣka from the year 25[23] to 60[24]. The earliest date for the next ruler Vāsudeva is known from the inscription as 64 or 67[25]. This would mean that Huviṣka's rule began some time between the year 23 and 25 and ended some time after the year 60 but before the year 64. Thus the reign period for Huviṣka, as known from these inscriptions, comes to approximately 40 years. Such a long period for a ruler, though not improbable, yet is not usual. As such, it has been the suspicion of many scholars that there might have been two rulers of the same name Huviṣka during this long period of 40 years. To support the existence of two Huviṣkas, during this period, Thomas, Basham and others[26] have placed their own arguments; and many of them are valid and sound in their own way. But none of them prove it positively. However, the coins, bearing the name Huviṣka, are demonstratively clear on this point, but unfortunately, to them, no serious attention has been given so far.

Excluding the two types of the gold coins, showing the king riding on the elephant and sitting cross-legged, which have just been shown above as belonging to Huviṣka I, the father of Kaniṣka I, there is only one type of gold coins of Huviṣka, which shows his bust in profile. The coins of this type uniformly show the king holding a mace or club in his right hand; but the object held by him in his left hand is not the same on all coins. It distinguishes the coins into two clear varieties. On some coins the king holds an *aṅkuśa* (goad) (*fig. 9*) and on others, he has a spear or sceptre, resting on his left shoulder (*fig. 10*). No historical interpretation of the coins of these two distinct varieties have so far been put forward. I venture to suggest that they relate to two different kings of the same name, Huviṣka (Huviṣka II and III), who were close to each other and were successive rulers.

We have a parallel instance in the Indo-Śaka coin series that bears the name Azes. All the coins uniformly show the king riding on horse to right; but on some of them, the king is seen holding a spear (*fig. 11*) and on others, he holds a whip (*fig. 12*). G.K. Jenkins has discussed these coins and has attributed them to two Azes — Azes I and II on the basis of the objects held by the horse-rider in his hand.[27] Azes I had spear in his hand and Azes II had the whip.

The suggestion of two Azes — I and II, based on the distinction of attributes in the hand of the king on the coins, has a conclusive support from the finds of the coins in two distinct layers in the excavations at Taxila. Unfortunately, no such excavational support is available to distinguish two Huviṣkas as suggested above. As a matter of fact it is extremely difficult to get gold coins as stray in any layer of an excavation, so one will have to depend on the evidence of coin-hoards, which are as valid and dependable as the evidences of coins found in excavational layers. Here in a hoard, found in 1965 in the district of Barabanki, Uttar Pradesh, there were 13 gold coins; and all of them were of Huviṣka. On everyone of them, the king is seen holding *aṅkuśa* (goad) in his left hand.[28] The hoard has none where the king holds spears or sceptre. Similarly, there is another hoard, which was discovered in 1971 in the district of Garhwal, Uttar Pradesh. It included 45 gold coins; 44 of them belonged to Huviṣka and the remaining one to Vāsudeva.[29] Here all the 44 coins of Huviṣka were of the type where the king holds spear or sceptre; on no coin in this hoard the king is noticed holding *aṅkuśa* (goad). The two hoards are so exclusive in their contents that they unmistakenly show that the two types of the coins of Huviṣka were issued distinctly in two different periods. They, thus, support the assumption that the coins relate to two different kings of the same name.

The association of the single coin of Vāsudeva in the Garhwal hoard, indicates that the spear (sceptre) type coins of Huviṣka were later, close to the time of Vāsudeva. This conclusion is confirmed from another hoard found in Meerut district, Uttar Pradesh.[30] Here the hoard included only one coin of Huviṣka and that of the spear (sceptre) type as the earliest; and all the other coins belonged to Vāsudeva and his successors. In the light of these two hoards, it may easily be concluded that the *aṅkuśa* (goad) type coins of Huviṣka would have been earlier. This conclusion is also supported by the Ahin Posh hoard of gold coins.[31] This hoard included along with the coins of Kaniṣka, a single coin of Huviṣka of the *aṅkuśa* (goad) type. These hoard evdences are enough to show that the *aṅkuśa* (goad) type coins were issued by Huviṣka II and the spear (sceptre) type by Huviṣka III.

Reference to MacDowall's observations about the weights of Huviṣka's copper coins[32] may again be made here. He has distinguished the second group of copper coins of Huviṣka into two classes, based on their weights. According to him, they represent the standards (i) 10 to 12 grammes and (ii) 7 to 9 grammes; and they belong to two distinct chronological phases, though he does not explicitly say that they belong to two kings. But in the light of what is discussed above, the copper coins of two different weight standards may well be attributed to two rulers — Huviṣka II and III, who succeeded one after the other.

Theory of Conjoint Rule—A Fallacy

Before we move to the post-Huviṣka period of the Kuṣāṇa history, it would be convenient to refer first to the theory of the conjoint rule of two rulers during the period of Huviṣka and his successor Vāsudeva, propounded by a number of scholars. This theory is based on the following inscriptions:

1. A Kharoṣṭhī inscription was found at Ārā, near Attack in Pakistan; it bears a line as *Maharajasa rajadirajasa devaputrasa kaisarasa Vajheṣkaputrasa Kaniṣkasya saṁvatsaraye 41.*[33] This

shows that there was a Kaniṣka, who was reigning in the year 41 (of the Kaniṣka or Kuṣāṇa era) and he was the son of Vajheṣka. This Kaniṣka is called by the scholars as Kaniṣka II.

2. A *yūpa* pillar was discovered at Īsāpur in Mathura district with the inscription *Mahārājasya Rajatirājasya Devaputrasya Ṣāhe Vaśiṣkasya rājye saṁvatsara caturviṁśa.*[34] This inscription discloses that a king named Vaśiṣka was ruling in the year 24 (of the Kaniṣka or Kuṣāṇa era).

3. Two inscribed Buddhist pedestals were discovered at Sanchī. They bear the name of Vaśiṣka with the dates 22[35] and 28[36].

Since the years 22 to 41, covered by all these inscriptions, are known also as the periods of Kaniṣka and Huviṣka, they appear overlapping them. So, the scholars have formulated a theory of co-rulership and have suggested that during the years 22 and 23 Vaśiṣka was co-ruler with Kaniṣka and thereafter with Huviṣka. And in the same vein, Kaniṣka of Ārā inscription is suggested to be the co-ruler with Huviṣka in the year 41.

To this theory, scholars of the Kuṣāṇa history have occasionally found something to add. For instance, a scholar has noticed an inscription on a pedestal of a Buddha image in the Indian Museum, Calcutta. There he has read the name of Kaniṣka and the date 34[37]. Since Kaniṣka I's reign was limited to the year 22 and Vaśiṣka was known as a co-ruler in the year 28, he has identified Kaniṣka of this inscription with Kaniṣka II; and thus he has narrowed down the co-rulership of Vaśiṣka along with Huviṣka to only a few years. Another scholar has tried to read the date 54 on another Mathura inscription bearing the name of Kaniṣka.[38] Being this date close to the Ārā inscription, he thought that Kaniṣka of both the inscriptions were identical. Another scholar has read the date of this very inscription as 94[39]. Since the period 34 to 94 for a ruler was a quite long one, he invented another Kaniṣka — Kaniṣka III as the co-ruler with Vāsudeva.

Conjoint rule of two rulers was quite prevalent amongst

the *Śaka* rulers of Afghanistan. They placed the names of the two rulers on the two sides of their coins. Co-rulership is also suggested amongst the Kṣatrapas of Western India. Both the rulers in this dynasty issued their coins simultaneously; but one of them always used a lower title. None of these two practice's is noticed on the coins of the Kuṣāṇa family. Since there is no other evidence to testify any system of conjoint rule, the suggestion of the conjoint rule amongst the Kuṣāṇas is merely assumptive. The hollowness of this fanciful theory was amply demonstrated by van Lohuizen in her *Scythian Period* as early as 1949; yet surprisingly enough, scholars are still clinched to it and repeat it on and off.

During the reign of the Kuṣāṇa rulers, between the years 2 and 98 large number of stone images were carved out at Mathura. A number of them bear inscriptions and mention dates. On the basis of the dates on these Mathura sculptures, van Lohuizen tried to reconstruct the relative chronology of the Mathura School of Art and focused attention to their stylistic characteristics. In course of her studies, several sculptures seemed to her anomalous from the artistic point. They showed elements which were much later than the dates mentioned on them. She clarified her point by referring to two Jain inscribed sculptures. One is dated in the 15th year of Kaniṣka and the other is dated in the year 86 in the reign of Vāsudeva. Both these sculptures refer in identical terms that they were erected at the instance of a Jain nun named Vasulā, who was the female disciple of another nun Saṅghamikā. It is unconceivable that the same lady occupied the same exalted position for more than 71 years. So, van Lohuizen carefully examined the stylistic characteristics of these two sculptures and arrived at the conclusion that the sculpture dated in the year 15 of Kaniṣka was later. She then suggested that the dating of these sculptures after the year 100 was renewed with 1; and 100 was omitted as was the practice in the Laukika era of Kashmir. She suggested that in the date 15, the figure of 100 was missing; and maintained that Kaniṣka of the sculpture bearing the date 15 was different from Kaniṣka I, whose dates are known from the year 2 to 22. She found support for the existence of this Kaniṣka in the post-Vāsudeva period from coins. Then she isolated some other sculptures bearing the name of Kaniṣka, ranging in date from 3 to 17 and attributed them to a later Kaniṣka, whom she called Kaniṣka III. This discovery was a great break through the Kuṣāṇa researches; but most unfortunate, it does not find proper attention at the hands of the historians.

Recently, Sarojini Kulshrestha, has made another startling discovery about the inscriptions of the Kuṣāṇas to which no attention was ever paid earlier.[40] She has pointed out that all the inscriptions of Kaniṣka I, Huviṣka and Vāsudeva up to the year 83 bear for them simply the title *Mahārāja rajatirāja Devaputra*;[41] but from the year 84 an additional title *Ṣāhi* is added to these titles for Vāsudeva.[42] This additional title is also seen along with the usual titles for Kaniṣka on the sculptures that van Lohuizen has attributed to the post-Vāsudeva period on the basis of their artistic peculiarities.[43] In the Allahabad pillar inscription of Samudragupta, the Kuṣāṇas that existed at that time are called *Daivaputra-Ṣāhi-Ṣāhānuṣāhi.*[44] Here also exists the additional title *Ṣāhi*. These inscriptions clearly indicate that an additional title *Ṣāhi* was added to the usual title *Mahārāja rajatirāja devaputra* for the Kuṣāṇas in the later part of Vāsudeva; and since then it became an integral part of the titles of the post-Vāsudeva rulers. The Kuṣāṇas were now recognised well by these titles by the time of Samudragupta.

In effect, this discovery brings out the historical fact that no inscription that has the additional title *Ṣāhi* for any Kuṣāṇa ruler, along with the usual titles, would or could be, in any way, earlier than the time of Vāsudeva. And this would ultimately mean that the Īsāpur *Yūpa* inscription and the Sanchi Buddhist Pedestal inscriptions, which bear the titles *Mahārāja rajatirāja Devaputra Ṣāhi* for Vaśiṣka, do not belong to the period of Kaniṣka I or Huviṣka and are of the post-Vāsudeva period and they are dated in the second Kaniṣka (Kuṣāṇa) era with 100 missing, to which van Lohuizen had drawn our attention. The existence of Vaśiṣka in the pre-Vāsudeva era thus vanishes like vapour in the air and the theory of conjoint rule crumbles into pieces. With this realization, Vajheṣka of the Ārā inscription would also be this Vaśiṣka and the date 41 as reckoned in the second Kaniṣka (Kuṣāṇa) era. At that time existed his son Kaniṣka.

Vāsudeva—More Than One

Now we come back to chronology. Huviṣka III was succeeded by Vāsudeva is clear from the coins of Garhwal and Meerut district hoards (discussed above). The Mathura inscriptions also testify the same. The latest inscription bearing the name of Huviṣka is dated 60[45] and the earliest of Vāsudeva is dated 64 or 67[46]. The inscriptions of the latter extend the date for him up to the year 98[47]. But as has been pointed out earlier, his inscriptions belonging to the period before the year 83 have for him only the titles *Mahārāja rajatirāja Devaputra*; and those that belong to the period later than 83 bear an additional title *Ṣāhi* for him. This distinctive appellation suggests the possibility of there being two rulers of the same name, who ruled one after the other.

This possibility gets support from the coins bearing the name Vāsudeva. They are distinguishable into two distinct types: (i) similar in fabric and contents as the coins of Kaniṣka and Huviṣka. They display the type -- standing king at altar on the obverse and Śiva standing in front of *nandi* (bull) on the reverse (*fig. 13*). These coins are well struck and neatly engraved. (ii) Similar to type (i) but a little different in style with an additional feature of trident-standard placed on the obverse in the left field (*fig. 14*). The introduction of this feature would not have been meaningless. So, on the basis of these two distinct types, Bachhofer had long back isolated two Vāsudevas, existing successively one after the other.[48]

The use of the title *Ṣāhi* in inscriptions and the introduction of trident-standard in the field on the coins, are two such distinctive features that, taken together, leave no doubt that there were two Vāsudevas — Vāsudeva I, whose inscriptions are known up to the year 83 without the *Ṣāhi* epithet for the ruler and who issued coins without the trident in the field; Vāsudeva II was he, who issued coins with trident-standard in the field and the inscriptions of his period had the title *Ṣāhi* for him. This Vāsudeva II existed from the year 84 to the year 98 (Kaniṣka or Kuṣāṇa era).

There is another type of coins bearing the name Vāsudeva. They are similar to the coins of Vāsudeva II in their motifs and contents; but are quite distinct from them in their fabric and execution. These coins are broad and thin and scyphate in their module. Moreover they have a *nandipada* symbol on the obverse in the right field (*fig. 15*). The use of the *nandipada* symbol here is a revival of the use, which is seen earlier for the last time on the coins of Vima Kadphises. On the reverse the deity *Oeṣo* (Śiva) has a lunar crescent at his forehead and frequently a halo. The legend of the obverse is frequently found blundered and the letters have begun to loose their legibility. The distinction between the letters *A* and *O, E* and *N* seems to be disappearing. These coins appear to be local, as they have mostly been found in Badakhshan, the region north of Hindu Kush and Seistan. Only a few coins are known from the Kabul region and Gandhāra and to their east. Whether these coins were issued by Vāsudeva II himself for the western part (west of Gandhāra) of his kingdom or his coins were imitated by someone else, needs probe, but it is not the subject of this paper. However, it may be added that similar coins were issued by the Sassanian governors, when they occupied this territory and called themselves *Kuśānaśāh.*

There is also a fourth type bearing the name Vāsudeva. They are in continuation, in respect of their fabric, to the coins of Vāsudeva II and have like them the trident-standard on the obverse in the left field; yet they are quite distinct from them. On them two new innovations are perceptible. Here the circular legend begins at 1 o'clock while on the earlier coins, it had its beginning from the time of Kaniṣka I at 7 o'clock. The second peculiarity here is the presence of a Brāhmī letter on the obverse in the right field and on the reverse close to the name of the deity (*fig. 16*). These peculiarities suggest the possibility of the existence of a third Vāsudeva within this period.

Post-Vāsudeva Kuṣāṇa Rulers

The territories west of Gandhāra were lost to the Sassanids, most likely, only in the time of Vāsudeva II; but the eastern Kuṣāṇa dominion, particularly the Yamuno-Gangetic region, was not affected in any way. It remained with them till the advent of the Gupta kings there. Of this period, the earliest are the three rulers, who are known from the inscriptions found on the Mathura sculptures, that are stylistically later and suggest their dates as reckoned in the second Kaniṣka (Kuṣāṇa) era:

Kaniṣka II year 5[49] to 17[50]

Vaśiṣka year 22[51] to 28[52]

Kaniṣka III year 3x or 32[53] to 41[54]

The existence of these three rulers is also attested from coins. Certain coins of the type of Vāsudeva II, having the standing king at the altar and a trident-standard in the left field on the obverse and Śiva with bull on the reverse, bear the circular inscription *ṢĀO NĀNO ṢAO KANEṢKO KOṢĀNO* (*fig. 17*). Here notable is that the name of the king is spelt as *Kaneṣko* and not *Kaneṣkī,* which is used on the coins of *Kaniṣka* I. Besides this distinction, these coins are very close to the coins, tentatively attributed here to Vāsudeva III. Like those coins, the circular legend here too begins at I and also have the single Brāhmī letter on the obverse and reverse. The issuer of these coins may well be taken as the successor of Vāsudeva III, if he existed, otherwise of Vāsudeva II. He may now be called Kaniṣka II, as there is no more hypothetical Kaniṣka II, who was so far being placed in the period of Huviṣka.

The coins of Vaśiṣka have come to our knowledge only some years back. They have been isolated by Göbl from amongst the coins that were so far been attributed to Vāsudeva. That was taken to be *Bazodeo* proved actually to be *Bazeṣko.* He noticed one such coin in the Peshawar Museum, another in the Ashmolean Museum, Oxford and two others in the British Museum, London.[55] But on all of them, the word *Bazeṣko* is truncated. The name *Bazeṣko,* in its full form and clear, is seen on a coin found in a hoard discovered in Jaunpur district, Uttar Pradesh (*fig. 20*), it is now deposited in the Lucknow Museum. Like the other coins, this coin too was originally attributed to Vāsudeva.[56] Later, B.N. Mukherjee drew attention to its correct identification.[57] These coins are very close to the coins of Kaniṣka II in their fabric and execution; and the obverse circular legend similarly begins on them at 1 o'clock. But on the reverse the motif is entirely different. Here is seen the goddess Ardokṣo seated on a high backed throne holding a cornucopiae in the left hand and a *pāśa* (noose) in the right hand (*figs. 19-20*). Ardokṣo is a well-known deity on the coins of Kaniṣka I and Huviṣka; but there she is seen invariably standing to right or left. In the present form, she is unknown on any earlier coin. Ardokṣo seated on throne appears to have been introduced first only on these coins of Vaśiṣka; and from now onwards it is constantly seen on the coins of his successors. From them the Gupta kings borrowed this motif for their early coins. Vaśiṣka of these coins may conveniently be identified with Vaśiṣka of Īsāpur *yūpa* and Sanchi pedestal inscriptions, where his name is associated with the title *Ṣāhi* along with the usual titles of the early Kuṣāṇas. He may also be identified with Vajheṣka of the Ārā inscription.

With the identification of Vajheṣka with Vaśiṣka it is naturally evident that his son Kaniṣka, whose date is known as 41, would be Kaniṣka III; and to him may be attributed all those Mathura inscriptions that are dated in the fourth decade of the Second Kaniṣka (Kuṣāṇa) era. He issued his coins on the pattern of the coins of his father Vaśiṣka, showing on the obverse the king at the altar, trident-standard on the left field and the circular legend beginning at 1 and on the reverse, the seated Ardokṣo. (*fig. 21*)

Then there is a series of coins, which are close to the coins of Kaniṣka III. They have Ardokṣo on the reverse seated on high backed throne; and on the obverse they retain the costume system of Kaniṣka III. But they are well distinguishable from the coins of Kaniṣka III. They have more exaggerated curve of hem of the tunic and a cruder and more conventionalised type of king's effigy. The bun of the hair of Kaniṣka III is absent on these coins. The circular legend on most of these coins is found missing. If it is ever noticed, it is found very much truncated to the extent of illegibility. In some rare cases, the first part of the legend may be made out as *Ṣāo Nāno Ṣāo*; and that too very much blundered. Scholars have conjectured that the tail part of the legend of these coins would have been *Kaneṣko* (or *Bazodeo*) *Koṣāno*. But it is difficult to subscribe to these conjectures. On these coins a word in Brāhmī letters is found under the left arm of the king. This word, so far noticed is *Vasu* on most coins (*fig. 22*) on some it is *Chara* or *Chū* (*fig. 23*) and on a few *Maśra* (*fig. 24*). On the coins of Maśra, the obverse legend begins at about XI óclock and is from outside. The Peculiarity of having a Brāhmī word under the left arm of the king, is also noticed on the Gupta gold coins, which are of a little later period. There too exists a word or a letter under the left arm of the king. Most likely the Guptas had borrowed this idea from these very Kuṣāṇa coins, when they adopted the entire pattern of the later Kuṣāṇa coins for their early coinage. On the Gupta coins this word or letter may easily be identified as representing the initial part of the name of the king, who issued them. In the light of the Gupta coins, it may be well surmised that the words on the Kuṣāṇa coins too would have been the initials of the Kuṣāṇa rulers, who issued them. These coins thus disclose that there existed at least three other Kuṣāṇa kings after Kaniṣka III, about whom the other sources are silent. The coins indicate that Maśra was the last amongst them; we are not sure of the order of succession of the other two Vasu and Chara.

On the coins having the name Vasu, some scholars have tried to see the name *Bazodeo* in the circular legend; and they attribute the coins to Vāsudeva, whom they identify as Vāsudeva II or III. These scholars have failed to realise that there is no medial sign for *ā* over *va* in the Brāhmī inscription to take it as any initial part of the name Vāsudeva. If *deva* was suffixed to it, it would only be Vasudeva and never Vāsudeva. Any Indian layman knows well that the names Vasudeva and Vāsudeva do not mean the same. The two names represent two different personalities. Vasudeva was the name of the father of Kṛṣṇa; and Kṛṣṇa was called Vāsudeva after the name of his father. Had the coins been issued by any Vāsudeva, the die-engraver would have not ignored the medial sign for *ā* over the letter *va*. So, these coins cannot be attributed to any Vāsudeva, in spite of the spelling *BAZODEO* (if it exists at all) in the circular Graeco-Bactrian script. In this script there was nothing to differentiate *va* from *vā*. As such this coin belongs to one whose name began with *Vasu*; the full name might be anything like Vasudeva, Vasumitra, Vasusena or it might be complete in itself.

The coins bearing the name Maśra are quite new to the scholars of Kuṣāṇa history and numismatics. They have come to light only recently with the discovery of the Jhunjhunu hoard of Later Kuṣāṇa gold coins.[58] Besides the coin found in this hoard, I have located two other specimens; one is in the Bhārat Kalā Bhavan, the Art and Archaeology Museum of the Benaras Hindu University and the other in the State Museum, Lucknow. Both of them are still unpublished. These coins are distinct from all other Kuṣāṇa coins. Here a *cakra* (wheel)-topped standard is noticed in the left hand of the king in place of the usual trident-standard (*fig. 24*). *Cakra*-topped standard in the hand of the Kuṣāṇa king reminds us of the well-known *Cakradhvaja* type coins of Kācagupta of the Gupta dynasty (*fig. 25*). There too, the king holds a *cakra* (wheel)-topped standard in his left hand in the same way as we notice of these coins. This striking similarity between the coins of two rulers, belonging to two different dynasties, unmistakenly indicate that the two rulers existed quite close to each other; and Kācagupta borrowed this standard from the coins of Maśra. This would ultimately mean to the history that Maśra was perhaps the last Kuṣāṇa ruler, who existed quite close in time to Kācagupta, who was an early ruler of the Gupta dynasty.

Decline of the Kuṣāṇas

The decline of the Kuṣāṇas in the Yamuno-Gangetic region is vaguely suggested at the hands of the Yaudheyas or the Nāgas.[59]

But hardly any vestiges of the Yaudheyas are known in this area. No Yaudheya coin has so far been found here. Nāga coins are known only a few, scattered here and there; they afford no evidence of their existence in this region. In any case, there had been a great vacuum of more than a century in the history of this region between the decline of the Kuṣāṇas and the rise of the Guptas. Historians have skipped over this period; no attempt has so far been made to explain this vacuum or to fill up this gap.

In view all that is discussed above, the study of the finds of coin-hoards in this region throws an illuminating light on this neglected history. They are distinguishable into two clear goups. One group of the finds are known from all parts of the eastern Kuṣāṇa dominion. They include the coins only of the earlier Kuṣāṇa rulers — Vima Kadphises, Kaniṣka I and Huviṣka II and III. In most of them, the coins of Vāsudeva are found absent; only in a few cases, they are seen. The other group of finds have exclusively the coins of Vāsudeva and his successors. In a few rare cases, the coins of Huviṣka are seen with them. The finds of the latter group are mostly confined to Mathura and its surroundings. These finds indicate that by the time of Vāsudeva, the eastern part of the Kuṣāṇa empire had considerably shrank; but they continued their holds in Mathura and its surroundings from the time of Vāsudeva till the rise of the Guptas. They were never wiped out at any time earlier.

A big hoard of 86 gold coins was discovered as early as 1915 in the village Mithathal in the district of Hisar (Haryana State). The coins were kept in an earthen vessel, which was found while ploughing a field. Of them 26 were melted before the Government machinery could get hold of the find under the Treasure Trove Laws. Only 60 came into the hands of the officials. Of these 33 coins related to Samudragupta (according to the identification of that time; actually only 29 related to Samundragupta and 4 belonged to Kācagupta). The remaining 27 were identified as the issues of the Later Kuṣāṇas.[60] The only other information regarding this hoard, that was available till recently, was that it included a coin of Battle-axe Type of Samudragupta of a rare variety, showing him facing right. This rare coin was published in an exclusive note.[61] It is also mentioned by Altekar.[62] Later, while going through the *Annual Reports* of the Central Museum, Lahore, I came to know from the *Report* for the year 1915-16 that the hoard was examined by R.B. Whitehead and he prepared a brief note on it. According to his note, some notable coins in the hoard were: (a) a very fine piece of Samudragupta's Battle-axe Type, belonging to a variety of which only one specimen was previously known (the same coin, which finds mention in the note referred to above); (b) a coin of Samudragupta of *Aśvamedha* type; and (c) four coins of Kāca. Whitehead did not say anything about the other coins of Samudragupta and the coins that he identified as the coins of the Later Kuṣāṇas. The Museum's *Report* for the subsequent year, i.e., 1916-17, disclosed that 20 coins of the said hoard were acquired by the Museum. Amongst the 20 coins acquired by the Lahore Museum, 11 belonged to the Guptas and the other 9 were those that were attributed to the Later Kuṣāṇas. Of these, 7 coins of Samudragupta and all the 9 coins, attributed to the Later Kuṣāṇas, are illustrated on two plates in the *Report* but without any description or detail. However, the plates help in knowing the coins acquired by the Museum. The illustrations of the nine coins, attributed to the Later Kuṣāṇas in the Museum's *Report* disclose that the hoard included the coins of Vāsudeva II, Kaniṣka II and III, Vasu and Chara. Along with them were also the coins of Ṣaka. In the obverse and reverse motifs, the Ṣaka coins are very much the same as the coins of Kaniṣka III showing Ardokṣo on the reverse; but the circular Graeco-Bactrian legend is replaced by cursive Kuṣāṇo-Bactrian script, similar to that, which is seen on the Kuṣāṇo-Sassanian coins. It apparently looks like the repetition of 0000; and for this reason, it has been declared by Cunningham as illegible.[63] Here on these coins, on the obverse, outside the trident-standard held by the king is found the word *Ṣaka,* which is considered to be a tribal name. In the central field, i.e., below the arm of the king is the name *Mī.* The coins of *Ṣaka,* along with the coins of the Guptas, are known, besides the

Mithathal hoard, in two other small hoards discovered in Uttar Pradesh.[64] They show that the Ṣakas were contemporary to the Guptas and were existing somewhere on the borders of the Gupta empire, most likely in Haryana and Punjab. These Ṣakas are the same that are mentioned in the Allahabad Pillar inscription along with the Kuṣāṇas (*Daivaputra-Ṣahi-Ṣāhānuṣāhi)* as *Ṣaka-muruṇḍa*.

Another hoard of gold coins of the Later Kuṣāṇas was discovered in Jhunjhunu district of Rājasthan in 1973.[65] The exact content of this hoard is not known; but it included the coins of all the rulers represented in the Mithathal hoard along with the coins of Ṣaka. It also brought to light an unknown Later Kuṣāṇa king called Maśra. This hoard had no coins of the Guptas; but as had already been pointed out earlier, the coin of Maśra is very close to the coins of Kācagupta of the Gupta dynasty.

The Mithathal and Jhunjhunu hoards, taken together, make it amply clear that the Later Kuṣāṇa rulers were closely linked with the Guptas and there was no hiatus at any time in the history of Mathura and its surroundings between the rule of the Kuṣāṇas and the Guptas. The hoards have the coins of Vāsudeva at one end, of Samudragupta and Kācagupta at the other. In between there was an unbroken chain of seven or eight rulers — Vāsudeva II (and Vāsudeva III), Kaniṣka II, Vaśiṣka, Kaniṣka III, Vasu, Chara and Maśra.

The Epoch of the Kaniṣka (Kuṣāṇa) Era

The above findings, based on the coins and inscriptions, present a new shape to, the history of the Kuṣāṇas. This also provides an occasion to look afresh into the vexed problem of the beginning of the Kaniṣka (Kuṣāṇa) era.

The common belief from the beginning of the studies of the Kuṣāṇa history, had been that Kaniṣka was the founder of the *Śaka* era of A.D. 78. This era was used earliest by the Kṣatrapas of Western India from the second through the fourth century A.D. But the earliest epigraphic records, where the name of the era itself is used, are the inscriptions of the Cālukyas found round about Badāmī. This era had been popular only in South India. In North India, its use in inscriptions is rare; and those that are there, are very late. There is no cogent reason to associate this era with a dynasty, which reigned only in North India. Furthermore, the Kuṣāṇas by their race, were never Śakas. Had been so, it could have been reason to associate Kaniṣka with this era. Had the Kuṣāṇas any kind of hegemony over the Western Kṣatrapas, that could also have been reason to associate Kaniṣka with the era. But we have no evidence to this effect too. In absence of any of these reasons, the only argument that is always placed to associate the era of A.D. 78 with the Kuṣāṇas is that Kaniṣka was the only foreign ruler, who is known to have actually begun an era. Whatever arguments are placed in favour of this date, the basic fact is always ignored that this date leaves a big gap of more than one and a half centuries between the Kuṣāṇas and the Guptas in the Yamuno-Gangetic region; and this gap remains unaccounted. This was certainly not the period of any anarchy; it is unthinkable that there would have been no administrative authority during this period. Apart from the political vacuum, this date creates problem with the palaeographists and the art connoisseurs also. The palaeographists do not see any considerable distinction between the Brāhmī letters of the inscriptions of the Later Kuṣāṇa and the Early Gupta periods. The same is the case with the sculptures of Mathura of this period. Sculptures, relating to the period of both the dynasties have been found together at Kaṅkālī Ṭīlā, Mathura town. These sculptures of the two periods have many common stylistic features, also, and that put them side by side. In the cases of palaeography and art, both, it is unthinkable that they remained inactive for more than a century and there was no development. The closeness between the late Kuṣāṇa and early Gupta palaeography and art, makes it almost certain that there was not any considerable gap of time between the Kuṣāṇas and the Guptas. This should be enough to counter all the arguments that might be placed in favour of A.D. 78 as the beginning of the Kaniṣka (Kuṣāṇa) era.

In recent years, those scholars who have sensed the absurdity in the theory of A.D. 78 as the epoch of the Kaniṣka

(Kuṣāṇa) era, have suggested new dates for it in the second century A.D. A.D.128 is suggested by Sten Konow[66] and W.K. van Wijk[67] for it. Roman Ghirshman has theorised that Kaniṣka acceded to power in about A.D. 144.[68] A.K. Narain[69] assigns the period of reign between 103 and 125 A.D. and John M. Rosenfield[70] thinks that Kaniṣka came to throne sometime between A.D. 110 and 115. Some of the arguments that these scholars have put forward in favour of their dates, do have merits and they deserve consideration; but they lead us nowhere. None of them have any peg, from which one could move forward or backward to arrive at the final solution.

This peg may well be fixed as A.D. 319, the date of the beginning of the Gupta era. This is a firm point from which we may move backward to fix the beginning of the reign of Kaniṣka. First, we should look to the Allahabad Pillar Inscription of Samudragupta, an earlier ruler of the Gupta dynasty. It bears the phrase *Daivaputra Ṣāhi Ṣāhānuṣāhi,* in the context of a neighbouring friendly state. This phrase is exactly the same as the *Mahārāja rajatirāja Devaputra Ṣāhi,* that we find in the inscriptions of Vāsudeva II and his successors. This leaves no doubt that the phrase in the Allahabad Pillar Inscription meant the Later Kuṣāṇa contemporary ruler who existed then at Mathura. The numismatic and the epigraphic evidences, taken together, make it clear that the Kuṣāṇas existed in the Mathura region as a friendly neighbour till the time of Samudragupta.

Next, we have an inscription of Chandragupta II at Mathura, which is dated in the Gupta year 61 and the regnal year 5 of the King.[71] This is the earliest Gupta inscription at Mathura and thus it indicates, in unambiguous terms, the occupation of Mathura by the Guptas by A.D. 380.

From these two inscriptions, taken together, it may well be deduced that the termination of the Kuṣāṇa rule at Mathura would have taken place only a little earlier than A.D. 380, the date of Mathura inscription. It would not be much to the side of error, if it is presumed that it might have taken place in *circa* A.D. 370. This date would be a fixed point in the history of the Kuṣāṇas. If the beginning of the reign of Kaniṣka is worked out backward from this point, it would be much more near the accuracy than any of the suggestions so far made.

The termination of the reign of Vāsudeva II in about the year 100 of the Kaniṣka (Kuṣāṇa) era is almost certain. During these 100 years existed five rulers — Kaniṣka I, Huviṣka II and III and Vāsudeva I and II. This provides broadly a figure of twenty years as the reign period for each of these rulers. Relying on this average reign period, which is on the high side of the average reign period of the rulers of the Indian dynasties, if the reign period for the post-Vāsudeva II rulers is calculated, it would cover 120 years. This calculation would place the termination of the Kuṣāṇa rule in the east in *circa* 220 Kaniṣka (Kuṣāṇa) era. And this would be the same as *circa* A.D. 370, calculated earlier, based on the Gupta inscriptions. This would thus fix *circa* 150 the date for the beginning of the reign of Kaniṣka.

The date A.D. 150 is quite close to the date A.D. 144, that was proposed by me earlier at the Conference that was held in 1960 at London on the date of Kaniṣka.[72] On that occasion, I had based my conclusion on the study of the coinage of the local rulers of Northern India that existed in between the post-Mauryan and pre-Kuṣāṇa periods. This date was reviewed again by me at the Conference on Mathura Culture, organised by the American Institute of Indian Studies at Delhi.[73] The basis was the same but was dealt a little differently. The result was the same.

Both these dates A.D. 144 and 150, proposed by me, are by no means precise or absolute. Nevertheless they hold firm ground and are less hypothetical than any of the dates suggested earlier. If there is any error in these dates, it would be minimal. The dates for the epoch of the Kaniṣka (Kuṣāṇa) era, suggested by other scholars also are not at any long distance from these dates. Most of the arguments, that have been adduced in favour of those dates might, if properly reassessed, would fit well with the date suggested here.

References

1. G.R. Sharma, *Reh Inscription of Menander and the Indo-Greek Invasion of Gaṅgā Valley,* Allahabad, 1980, pp. 8-10.
2. T.P. Verma, A Note on the Reh Inscription. In *Raṅgavalli, Recent Researches in Indology,* Bombay, 1981, pp. 77-80.
3. B.N. Mukherjee, *Indian Museum Bulletin,* Calcutta, 1973, p. 114; K.W. Dobbins, *East and West,* Rome 25, 1975, pp. 105-09.
4. *Journal of the Epigraphical Society of India,* VII (1980), pp. 98-100.
5. The Hāthīgumphā inscription refers in line 8 to a *yavana-rāja,* who fled to Mathura when he realized the might of Khāravela. The name of the *yavana-rāja* bears 3 letters, of which, the second letter may be fairly read as *ma* or *mi.* It has been doubtfully restored as *Dimita,* meaning Demetrius, the Indo-Greek king. But as early as 1951, I thought it to be *Vimaka,* meaning Vima Kadphises. The Patna Museum has a plaster cast of this inscription, which I personally examined when I was there as Curator. It confirms my suggestion.
6. Compare with the figure on Ujjain coins. (*B.M.C.,A.I.,* pl. XXXVII, 1-4.)
7. *B.M.C.,A.I.,* pp. 191, Var. *b.*
8. Mathura Museum, No. 215A. *J.R.A.S.,* 1924, p. 401; V.S. Agrawala, *J.U.P.H.S.,* XXIII, 1950, pp. 40-41.
9. *A.S.I.,A.R.,* 1911-12, pp. 122 ff.; *E.I.,* XXI, p. 59; *J.U.P.H.S.,* XXIII, 1950, pp. 40-41.
10. That Vematakṣama was quite different from Vima Kadphises is clear from the fact that *takṣama* can in no way be equated with Kadphises either philologically or phoneticaly. Moreover, Vematakṣama bears the title *Mahārāja rajatirāja devaputra Kuṣāṇaputra Ṣāhi.* Vima Kadphises or any other Kuṣāṇa ruler is not called *Kuṣāṇaputra.* This epithet is exclusive to Vematakṣama. Then the title *Ṣāhi* was used only in the later period of Vāsudeva, as shown in this paper (supra, p. 171ff); and was used only by the post-Vāsudeva rulers. Thus *Vematakṣama* may be placed only in the later Kuṣāṇa period and not earlier.
11. *J.R.A.S.,* 1932, p. 116, Notes on the Scythic Period.
12. *Papers of the Date of Kaniṣka,* p. 46.
13. A. Stein (trans.), *Rājataraṅgiṇī,* I, 168-73.
14. Kankali Tila Jain Image, Lucknow, Museum: *E.I.,* II, p. 205; *J.R.A.S.,* 1903, p. 352; *I.A.,* XXXIII, p. 38.
15. *J.R.A.S.,* 1915, pp. 108-16.
16. *B.S.O.A.S.,* XX 1950, p. 77-78.

17. *J.N.S.I.*, XXII, p. 99.
18. *Ibid.*, XX, pp. 162-71.
19. *Ibid.*, XXII, pp. 71-73.
20. *Ibid.*, p. 71.
21. Kauśāmbī Bodhisattva image, Allahabad Museum, No. 2948; *E.I.*, XXIV, p. 211.
22. Sonkh Buddhist image, Mathura Museum No. 1602; *J.R.A.S.*, 1924, p. 400; *J.U.P.H.S.*, XXI, 1948, pp. 45-46.
23. Govindnagar Buddha image inscription, now in Mathura Museum.
24. Kankali Tila Jain image, Lucknow Museum No. J26: *E.I.*, I, p. 346; *I.A.*, XXXIII, p. 105.
25. Buddhist pedestal inscription Mathura Museum No. 2906; *P.I.H.C.* 1941, pp. 163-64; *El*, XXX, pp. 181-84.
26. *Supra*, fn. 13-16.
27. *J.N.S.I.*, XVII, pp. 1 ff.; *T.I.N.C.*, 1957, pp. 123 ff.
28. *Ibiḍ*, XXXI, p. 15.
29. *Ibiḍ*, XXXVI, pp. 72 ff.
30. Unpublished; in State Museum, Lucknow. Examined by me.
31. *P.A.S.B.*, 1897, pp. 122 ff.; 205.
32. *J.N.S.I.*, XXII, p. 72.
33. S. Konow, *Corpus Inscriptionum Indicarum*, I, pp. 165 ff.
34. Mathura Museum No. Q13; *J.R.A.S.*, 1910, p. 1311; *A.S.I.,A.R.*, 1910-11, pp. 40-48; *J.U.P.H.S.*, XXIV, 1951, p. 136.
35. Sanchi Museum No. A. 83; Marshall, *Monuments of Sanchi*, p. 386, Pl. 105c.
36. Sanchi Museum No. A. 82; Marshall *ibid.*, p. 385, Pl. 124b.
37. *Mathura Inscriptions*, pp. 199-200; *E.I.*, XIX, p. 65-66.
38. *E.I.*, XXVI, pp. 293-97.
39. B.N. Mukherjee, *The Kuṣāṇa Genealogy*, pp. 71-72; D.C. Sircar, *PAIOC*, XII, 1943-44, p. 521.
40. Sarojini Kulashreshtha, *N.D.* X; 1986, pp. 71-75.; supra, pp. 137-146.
41. KANIṢKA. Mat portrait sculpture, Mathura Museum No. 213, *A.S.I.,A.R.*, 1911-12, p. 122 ff.; *J.U.P.H.S.*, XXIII, 1950, pp. 39-40. Sravasti Bodhisattva, Indian Museum: *E.I.*, XIII, p. 180; IX, p. 291. Inscription dated 10, British Museum, 1888, 7-15.53: *E.I.*, IX, pp. 239-41.

    HUVIṢKA. Chaubara Buddhist Image, Lucknow Museum No. B. 2: *I.A.*, VI, p. 217; XXXIII, p. 39. Kankali Tila Jain Image, Lucknow Museum: *E.I.*, II,

p. 206; *J.R.A.S.*, 1903, p. 262. Lakhanu Bodhisattva, Mathura Museum No. A63: *J.U.P.H.S.*, XXI, 1948, p. 47. Kankali Tila Elephant Capital: Cunningham, *A.S.R.* II, p. 32: *I.A.*, XXXIII, p. 40. Mat Portrait Pedestal, Mathura Museum No. 215A: *J.R.A.S.*, 1929, p. 401; *J.U.P.H.S.*, XXIII, 1950, p. 132. Buddhist Image, Bombay University: *J.B.B.R.A.S.*, XX, p. 289. Buddhist Image dated 50, Mathura Museum No. B79: *J.U.P.H.S.*, XXIII, 1950, p. 3. Jamalpur Buddhist Image, Lucknow Museum No. B3: *J.A.S.B.*, XLVIII, p. 130; *E.I.*, X. p. 12. Naroli Buddhist Pedestal, Mathura Museum No. 3622: *Siksha*, April 1955, pp. 136-37. Kankali Tila Jain Image, Lucknow Museum No. J26: *E.I.*, I, p. 381; *I.A.*, XXXIII, p. 105.

VĀSUDEVA. Jamalpur Stone Slab dated 74, Indian Museum: *E.I.*, I, p. 373; IX, p. 241; *I.A.*, XXXIII, p. 106.

42. Balbhadra Kund Jain Image dated 84, Mathura Museum No. B4: *J.U.P.H.S.*, XXIII, 1950, p. 6. Kankali Tila Jain image dated 87: Cunningham, *ASR*, III, p. 35; *I.A.*, XXXIII, p. 108.

43. Kankali Tila Jain Image dated year 7, Lucknow Museum No. J6: *E.I.*, I, p. 391. Nāgarāja Relief dated year 8, Mathura Museum No. 211: *E.I.*, XVII, p. 10; *J.U.P.H.S.*, XXIII, 1950, p. 103. Kankali Tila Jain Image dated 17, Mathura Museum No. 3383: Unpublished.

44. Fleet, *C.I.I.*, III. p. 14, L. 8.

45. Kankali Tila Jain Image, Lucknow Museum J. 26: *E.I.*, I, p. 386; *I.A.*, XXXIII, p. 105.

46. Buddhist Pedestal Inscription, Mathura Museum No. 2907: *E.I.*, XXX, pp. 181-84.

47. Kankali Tila Jain Image: Cunningham, *A.S.R.*, III, p. 35; *I.A.*, XXXIII, p. 108.

48. *J.A.O.S.*, LVI, 1936, pp. 429-39.

49. Kankali Tila Jain Image, Lucknow Museum No. J3: *E.I.*, II, p. 201; *I.A.*, XXXIII, p. 264.

50. Kankali Tila Jain Image, Mathura Museum No. 3385: Unpublished.

51. Sanchi Buddhist Pedestal, Sanchi Museum No. A83: Marshall, *Monuments of Sanchi*, p. 356.

52. Sanchi Buddhist image, Sanchi Museum No. A82: Marshall, *ibid.*, p. 385.

53. B.N. Mukherjee, *The Kuṣāṇa Genealogy*, pp. 77-78.

54. Ārā Inscription: *C.I.I.*, I, p. 165.

55. *Dokumente zur Geschichte der iranische Hunnen in Baktrien und Indien*, Vol. II, pp. 308; 312-13.

56. *B.M.A.U.P.*, No. 4, Dec. 1969, p. 28. fig. 12.

57. *J.N.S.I.*, XXXIV, pp. 31 ff.

58. *N.D.* V, p. 34.
59. Altekar & Majumdar, *Gupta-Vakataka Age*, pp. 28, 37-38.
60. *A.S.I.,A.R.*, 1915-16, p. 19.
61. *Ibid.*, 1916-17, pp. 233-34.
62. *The Coinage of the Gupta Empire*, p. 309.
63. *Later Indo Scythians*, repr. 1962, p. 28.
64. A.K. Srivastava, *Coin-hoards of Uttar Pradesh*, Entries 7 and 1130.
65. *N.D.*, V.ii, pp. 25ff.
66. *Acta Orientalia*, III, 1924, pp. 52-91.
67. *Ibid.*, V, 1927, pp. 168-70.
68. *JA*, 1943-45, pp. 59-71; *Begram*, Mémoires de la Delegation Archéologique Francaise en Afghanistan, Vol. 12, Cairo, 1946; *Cahiers d'historie mondiale*, III, 1957, pp. 689-721.
69. *Papers on the Date of Kanishka*, p. 221.
70. *The Dynastic Arts of the Kuṣāṇas*, Berkeley & Los Angeles, 1967, pp. 257-58.
71. *E.I.*, XXI, p. 190; *I.H.Q.*, XVIII, p. 171.
72. *Papers on the Date of Kanishka*, pp. 119; supra, p. 55ff.
73. *Mathura : The Cultural Heritage*, Ed. Davis M. Srinivasan, New Delhi 1989, pp. 132-135; supra, p. 144ff..

Bibliography

Acharya, P., Ancient Coins from Mayrubhanj, In *J.N.S.I.*, II, pp. 125-26.

Allan, J., *Catalogue of Indian Coins in the British Museum, Ancient India,* London, 1936.

Alteker, A.S., *Coinage of the Gupta Empire,* Varanasi, 1957.

——, New Kings and Interesting Coin-types of Kausambi. In *J.N.S.I.*, II, p. 1-16.

——, A Unique Kuṣāṇa-Roman Gold coin of King Dharmadamadhusa (?). In *J.N.S.I.*, XII, p. 1-4.

——, Coins of Kumrahar and Bulandibagh Excavations. In *J.N.S.I.*, XIII, p. 143-44.

——, A Golden Amulet imitating a gold coin of Huviṣka. In *J.N.S.I.*, XX, pp. 1-3.

——, Buxar Hoard of Kuṣāṇa Coins. In *J.N.S.I.*, XXX, pp. 21-23.

——, *Kumrahar Excavations: 1951-55,* Patna.

Altekar, A.S. and Majumdar, R.C., *The Vakataka-Gupta Age,* Reprint, Varanasi, 1954.

Ancient India, Archaeological Survey of India.

Annotated Bibliography of Central Soviet Archaeology and Kuṣāṇa Culture, Dashambe, 1968.

Annual Report of the Mysore Archaeological Department.

Arvamuthan, T.G., *Venecian Coins in the Government Museum,* Madras.

Bachhofer, L., Herrscher und Munzen der Spaten Kuṣāṇas. In *J.A.O.S.*, LVI, pp. 429-39.

Banerji, A., Ancient and Medeival Coins of Orissa. In *J.N.S.I.*, IX, pp. 105-10.

——, Eastern Expansion of the Kuṣāṇa Empire. In *I.H.Q.*, XVIII, pp. 294-303.

——, Kuṣāṇas in Eastern India. In *J.N.S.I.*, XIII, pp. 107-09.
Banerji, R.D., *History of Orissa.*
——, New Brahmi Inscriptions of the Scythian Period. In *E.I.*, X, 106-21.
——, Notes on Indo-Schythan Coinage. In *J.A.S.B.*, IV, 1908, pp. 81-93.
Basham, A.L., *Papers on the Date of Kaniṣka,* Leiden, 1968.
——, The Succession of the Line of Kaniṣka, In *B.S.O.A.S.*, XX, pp. 77-88.
Behra, K.S., On a Kuṣāṇa Coin from Orissa. In *J.N.S.I.*, XXXVII, pp. 67-72.
Behra, S.C., A Find of Puri-Kuṣāṇa Coins in Bhillingi. In *J.N.S.I.*, XXXII, pp. 23-34.
Blotch, T., Two Inscriptions on Buddhist Images. In *E.I.*, VIII, pp. 161ff.
Buddhist Antiquities of Nāgārjunikoṇḍā.
Buhler, G., Further Jain Inscriptions from Mathura. In *E.I.*, pp. 206.
——, Further Votive Inscriptions of Sanchi. In *E.I.*, II, pp. 269ff.
——, New Jain Inscriptions from Mathura. In *E.I.*, I, pp. 286ff.
Chattopadhyay, B., *The Age of the Kuṣāṇas,* Calcutta, 1967.
Chaudhury, R.K., Gold Coins and Gold Image from Sultanganj. In *I.N.C.*, II, pp. 81-83.
Cunningham, A., *Coins of Indo-Schythic, Śakas and Kuṣāṇas,* Reprint, Varanasi, 1971.
——, Kaṅkali Ṭilā Jain Image. In *C.A.S.R.*, III, p. 35
——, *Mahabodhi.*
Dar, M.B.L., Some Rare Pañcāla Coins from the Site of Ahichchhatra. In *J.N.S.I.*, II, pp. 115ff.
Deo, S.B. & Gupte, R.S. *Excavations at Bhokardan* 1973, Nagpur, 1974.
Explorations at Karad.
Fleet, J.F., *Corpus Inscriptionum Indiacarum,* III.
Ganguly, D.K., The Imperial Kuṣāṇa Coins and their Imitations in Orissa. In *J.N.S.I.*, XXVIII, pp. 6-11.
Ghirshman, R., *Begram, Reserches Archaeogique et historique sur les Kouchens,* Memoires de la delegation Archaelogique Francaise en Afghanistan, Cairo, 1948.

Göbl, R., *Munzprägung des Kušānreiches,* Wein, 1981.

Goswami, K.G., Kosam Inscription of the reign of Kaniṣka, of the year 2. In *E.I.,* XXIV, pp. 211.

Gupta, P.L., Eastern Expansion of the Kuṣāṇa Empire. In *I.H.Q.* XXIX, pp. 205-22.

——, Date of Kuṣāṇa Currency in Eastern India. In *J.N.S.I.,* XV, pp. 185-92.

——, A Kausambi Copper Coin of Indradeva. In *J.N.S.I.,* XXI, pp. 64-67.

——, Gold Amulet and Kuṣāṇa History. In *J.N.S.I.,* XXI, pp. 188-93.

——, A Kuṣāṇa Coin with Brahmi Legend. In *J.N.S.I.,* XXXV, pp. 123-25.

——, Kuṣāṇa-Muruṇḍa Rule in Eastern India. In *J.N.S.I.,* XXXVI, pp. 25-53.

——, A Coin Hoard from Kausambi. In *J.N.S.I.,* XXXVIII, pp. 46-57.

——, British Museum Romano-Kuṣāṇa Medallion: Its Nature and Importance. In *J.N.S.I.,* XXXVIII, ii, pp. 73-81.

——, The Coinage of the Local Kings of Northern India and the Date of Kaniṣka. In *Papers on the Date of Kaniṣka,* Leiden, 1968, pp. 114-20.

——, *The Imperial Guptas,* Varanasi, 1971.

——, Chronology of the Post-Kuṣāṇa Rulers and the Allied Tribes. In *K.P. Jayaswal Commemoration Volume,* Patna 1981, pp. 291-99.

——, Early Coins of Mathura Region. In *Mathura: The Cultural Heritage,* New Delhi, 1989, pp. 130-38.

——, Kuṣāṇas in the Yamuno-Gangetic Region: Chronology and Date. In *Annali,* Instituto Universitario Orientale, Naples Italy, 45, pp. 199-222.

Haig, T.W. & Dodwell, H.H., *Cambridge History of India,* I Cambridge, 1934.

Jain, B.C., Kuṣāṇa Coins from Madhya Pradesh. In *J.N.S.I.,* XVII, p. 109.

——, A Hoard of 757 Kuṣāṇa Copper Coins from Sahdol District of Madhya Pradesh. In *J.N.S.I.,* XXVII, pp. 128-29.

——, Kuṣāṇa Coins from Sahdol District. In *J.N.S.I.*, XXVIII, pp. 1-5.

Konow, S., *Corpus Inscriptionum Indicarum*, I.

——, Ārā (Kharoṣthi) Inscription. In *E.I.*, XIV, pp. 130-43.

——, Mathura Brahmi Inscription of the Year 28, XXI, pp. 55-58.

Kulshreshtha, S., Coins of Vāśiṣka-Historical Implications. In *N.D.*, X, pp. 70-80.

——, Quarter-Stater of Kaniṣka. In *N.D.*, VII, ii, pp. 23-24; IX, pp. 46-51.

Levi, S., Notes on Indo-Scythians. In *I.A.*, XXXII, pp. 380-82.

Lohuizen de Leeu, J.V. Van, *The Sythian Period*. Leiden, 1949.

Luders, H., The Early Brahmi Inscription. In *E.I.*, II, pp. 101-09.

——, Epigraphic Notes. In *I.A.*, XXXII, pp. 33-41; 101-09.

MacDowall, D.W., The Weight Standard of the Gold and Copper Coins of the Kuṣāṇa Dynasty from Vima Kadphises to Vāsudeva. In *J.N.S.I.*, XXIV, pp. 71-75.

Maity, S.K., The Gold Contents of the Kuṣāṇa, the Kuṣāṇa Chiefs and the Sassanian Gold Coins from the Indian Museum, Calcutta. In *J.N.S.I.*, XX, pp. 162-71.

Majumdar, R.C., *Ancient India*.

Marshall, J., *The Monuments of Sanchi*, Calcutta, 1940.

Misra, Y. & Roy, S.R., *Guide to Vaisali and Vaisali Museum*, Patna, 1969.

Mukherji, B.N., A Gold Coin of Bazeṣka. In *J.N.S.I.*, XXXIV, pp. 31-35.

——, An Interesting Coin from Sonkh, Mathura. In *A.S.M.B.*, II, 8, p. 6.

——, *The Kuṣāṇa Geneology*, Calcutta, 1957.

——, *The Kuṣāṇas and the Deccan*, Calcutta, 1968.

Narain, A.K., Numismatic Evidence and Historical Writings. In *J.N.S.I.*, XVIII, ii, pp. 157-63.

——, A Unique Gold and Two Silver Coins of Huviṣka. In *J.N.S.I.*, XXVI, pp. 97-101.

——, Coin Hoards from Bihar. In *I.N.C.*, VIII, pp. 45-110.

Prasad, H.K., Coin Hoards from Orissa, In *I.N.C.*, VI, pp. 63-71.

Pokharna, P., A Hoard of Gold Coins from Rajasthan. In *J.N.S.I.*, XXXIX, p. 160.

——, Later Kuṣāṇa Coins from Rajasthan. In *N.D.*, V. ii, pp. 25-35.

Puri, K.N., *Exacavations at Rairh, 1939-40,* Jaipur.

Ramchandran, T.N., Find of Puri-Kuṣāṇa or Oriya-Kuṣāṇa coins from Sitabhanji. In *J.N.S.I.*, XIII, pp. 69-72.

Rhys Davids, *Buddhist India,* Calcutta, 1957.

Rockhill, W.A., *The Life of Buddha.*

Rosenfield, J.M., *The Dynastic Arts of the Kuṣāṇas,* Los Angles, 1967.

Sahni, D.R., Mathura Pedestal Inscription of the Kaniṣka Year 14. In *E.I.*, XIX, pp. 96-97.

——, Seven Stone Inscriptions from Mathura. In *E.I.*, XIX, pp. 65-69.

——, Three Mathura Inscriptions and on their bearing on the Kuṣāṇa Dynasty. In *J.R.A.S.*, 1924, pp. 399-406.

Sankalia, H.D., *Excavations at Brahmapuri,* Pune,

Sharma, G.R., *Reh Inscription of Menander and the Indo-Greek Invasion of the Ganga Valley,* Allahabad, 1984.

Sinha, B.P. & Roy., S.R., Vaisali Excavations, 1951-62, Patna, 1969.

Sircar, D.C., *Select Inscriptions. Bearing on Indian History and Civilisation,* I, Calcutta, 1942, 1960.

Singh, S.P., Numismatic Evidence of Kuṣāṇa-Muruṇḍa Rule in Eastern India. In *J.N.S.I.*, XXXV, pp. 127-41.

Smith, V.A., *Catalogue of Coins in the Indian Museum,* I, Oxford, 1906.

Sohoni, S.V., Finds at Sultanganj. In *I.N.C.*, I, p. 86.

Srinivasan, D.W., *Mathura: the Cultural Heritage,* New Delhi, 1984.

Srivastava, A.K., Find Spots of Kuṣāṇa Coins in U.P. In *B.M.A.U.P.*, 8, p. 81.

——, A Hoard of Kuṣāṇa Coins from Jaunpur District. In *B.M.A.U.P.*, No. 4, pp. 27-30.

——, Kuṣāṇa Coins from Barabanki. In *J.N.S.I.*, XXXI, pp. 15-21.

——, Kuṣāṇa Coins from Garhwal. In *J.N.S.I.*, XXXVII, pp. 72-73.

Srivastava, C.S., Coin Hoards of Treasure Trove Coins from U.P. In *B.M.A.U.P.*, 8, pp. 48-67.

Stein, A., *Kalhaṇa's Rājataraṅgiṇī.*

Tarn, W.W., *Greeks in Bactria and India.*

Thomas, F.W., Notes on Scythic Period. In *J.R.A.S.*, 1952, pp. 116ff.

———, *Tibetan Literary Texts and Documents concerning Chinese Turkistan*, London, 1935.

Verma, T.P., A Note on the Reh Inscription, In *Raṅgavalī, Recent Researches in Indology*, Bombay 1981, pp. 77-80.

———, A Quarter Stater of Kaniṣka. In *J.N.S.I.*, XLV, pp. 36-37.

Vogel, Ph. J., The Sacrificial Post of Isapur. In *A.S.I.,A.R.*, 1911-12, pp. 122ff.

Wakankar, V.S., Graceo-Roman Bullae from Ujjain. In *J.N.S.I.*, XXXII, pp. 211-14.

Whitehead, R.B., *Catalogue of Coins in the Punjab Museum, I, Lahore*, I, Oxford, 1914.

Wilson, H.H., *Ariana Antiqua*, London 1841.

Index

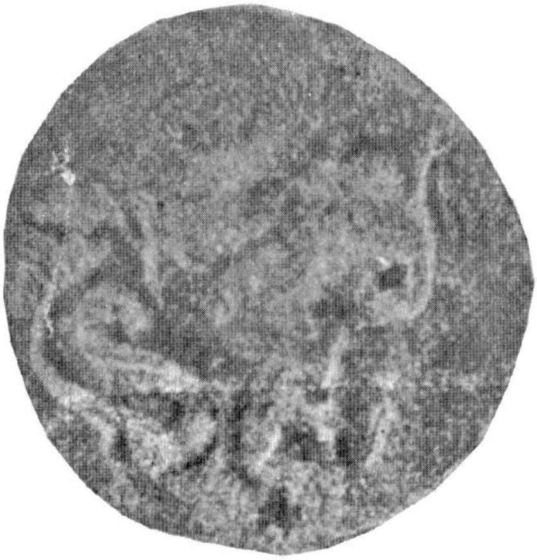

fig. 1 (a)

fig. 1 (b)

fig. 2 (a)

fig. 2 (b)

fig. 3

fig. 4

fig. 5

fig. 6

fig. 1 (a & b) Copper coin of Vima Kadphises, countermarked with Afrigid *Tamghā* (Obverse and Reverse)

fig. 2 (a & b) Copper coin of Kaniṣka (I) son of Huviṣka (Obverse and Reverse)

fig. 3 Gold coin of Huviṣka, Elephant-rider (Obverse)

fig. 4 Gold coin of Huviṣka – Seated cross-legged (Obverse)

fig. 5 Gold coin of Vima Kadphises – Elephant-rider (Obverse)

fig. 6 Gold coin of Vima Kadphises – Seated cross-legged (Obverse)

fig. 7

fig. 8

fig. 9

fig. 10

fig. 11

fig. 12

fig. 13 (a)

fig. 13 (b)

fig. 7 Gold coin of Huviṣka (Reverse) showing Monogram 1

fig. 8 Gold coin of Huviṣka (Reverse) showing Monogram 2

fig. 9 Gold coin of Huviṣka holding *aṅkuśa* (Obverse)

fig. 10 Gold coin of Huviṣka holding sceptre or standard (Obverse)

fig. 11 Silver coin of Indo-Śaka ruler Azes I, holding spear (Obverse)

fig. 12 Silver coin of Indo-Śaka ruler Azes II, holding whip (Obverse)

fig. 13 (a & b) Gold coin of Vāsudeva I – (Obverse and Reverse)

fig. 14 (a)

fig. 15 (a)

fig. 16 (a)

fig. 14 (b)

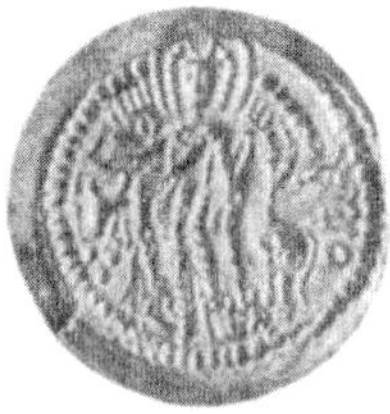

fig. 15 (b)

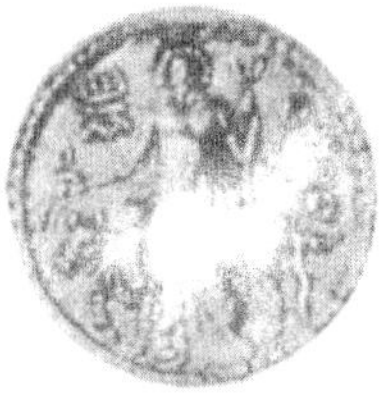

fig. 16 (b)

fig. 17 (a)

fig. 18 (a)

fig. 18 (b)

fig. 17 (b)

fig. 18 (c)

fig. 18 (d)

fig. 14 (a & b) Gold coin of Vāsudeva II – Trident in field (Obverse and Reverse)

fig. 15 (a & b) Gold coin of Vāsudeva (Scyphate) (Obverse and Reverse)

fig. 16 (a & b) Gold coin of Vāsudeva (ḷetter in margin) (Obverse and Reverse)

fig. 17 (a & b) Gold coin of Kaniṣka II – Oesho reverse (Obverse and Reverse)

fig. 18 (a & b) Gold quarter-stater of Kaniṣka (Original size and 18 c-d

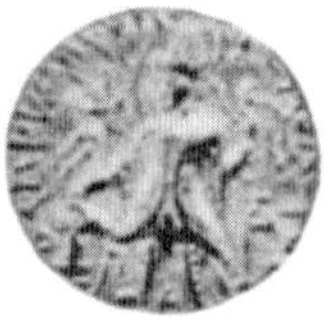

fig. 19 (a)

fig. 19 (b)

fig. 20 (a)

fig. 20 (b)

fig. 21 (a)

fig. 21 (b)

fig. 22 (a)

fig. 22 (b)

fig. 19 (a & b) Gold coin of Vāśiṣka, British Museum (Obverse and Reverse)

fig. 20 (a & b) Gold coin of Vāśiṣka, Delhupur hoard in Lucknow Museum (Obverse and Reverse)

fig. 21 (a & b) Gold coin of Kaniṣka III – Ardokso reverse (Obverse and Reverse)

fig. 22 (a & b) Gold coin of Later Kuṣāṇa Vasu (Obverse and Reverse)

fig. 23 (a)

fig. 23 (b)

fig. 24 (a)

fig. 24 (b)

fig. 25 (a)

fig. 25 (b)

fig. 23 (a & b) Gold coin of Later Kuṣāṇa Chara (Obverse and Reverse)

fig. 24 (a & b) Gold coin of Later Kuṣāṇa Masra (Obverse and Reverse)

fig. 25 (a & b) Gold coin of Gupta King Kāchagupta (Obverse and Reverse)

fig. 26 (a)

fig. 26 (b)

fig. 27 (a)

fig. 27 (b)

fig. 28 (a)

fig. 28 (b)

fig. 26 (a & b) Copper Kuṣāṇa coin with name Vīra (Obverse and Reverse)

fig. 27 (a & b) Imitation copper Kuṣāṇa coin (Obverse and Reverse)

fig. 28 (a & b) Imitation copper Kuṣāṇa coin (Obverse and Reverse)

fig. 29 (a & b) Romano-Kuṣāṇa gold m̃edallion (Obverse and Reverse)

fig. 30 Swedish gold medallion, Stockholm Museum (Front)

fig. 31 Reh (Fatehpur) Inscription of Vima Kadphises.